LISA C

REVEAL THE GIFT

LIVING THE FEMININE GENIUS

ASCENSION

West Chester, Pennsylvania

Nihil obstat: David N. Uebbing, MA, BA
                   Censor librorum

Imprimatur: +Most Reverend Samuel J. Aquila, STL
                 Archbishop of Denver
                 November 29, 2021

Ascension
PO Box 1990
West Chester, PA 19380
1-800-376-0520
ascensionpress.com

Cover design: Rosemary Strohm

Printed in the United States of America
22 23 24 25 26 5 4 3 2 1
ISBN 978-1-954881-26-6

Dedication

To my husband, Kevin:
Thank you for always encouraging me to live from my genius.

Necessary emphasis should be placed on the "genius of women," not only by considering great and famous women of the past or present, but also those ordinary women who reveal the gift of their womanhood by placing themselves at the service of others in their everyday lives. For in giving themselves to others each day women fulfill their deepest vocation.

–St. John Paul II

CONTENTS

Introduction 1

Chapter 1: Can I Get a Definition, Please? 5

Chapter 2: Self-Giving and St. Edith Stein 21

Chapter 3: Receptivity and Servant of God
Chiara Corbella Petrillo 35

Chapter 4: Maternity and St. Elizabeth Ann Seton 47

Chapter 5: Sensitivity and Servant of God Dorothy Day . . 61

Chapter 6: Intuition and St. Catherine of Siena 77

Chapter 7: Generosity and Servant of God Julia Greeley . . 91

Chapter 8: Fidelity and the Women at the Cross 105

Chapter 9: Strength and the Women
of the French Revolution .119

Chapter 10: The Ideal Woman 135

Conclusion 151

Epilogue. 155

Appendix 157

Bibliography 163

Acknowledgments 167

Introduction

About ten years ago, I received an entirely unwarranted invitation to speak to four thousand women on the topic of authentic Catholic femininity. The invitation came for FOCUS' SEEK conference, one of the largest Catholic young adult conferences offered globally. At the time, my husband and I were missionaries with FOCUS (the Fellowship of Catholic University Students), so the selection committee knew me. Honestly, though, I thought they were crazy for extending this request.

I had never before spoken on the topic of femininity, let alone *authentic Catholic* femininity. I knew next to nothing about what one would say regarding such a daunting and heavily debated topic. Furthermore, when it came to the whole "womanhood thing," I felt like I was a mediocre example of what a woman should be. I was pretty sure I was failing at being one every single day.

This "Girl Thing"

Growing up, I was not much of a stereotypical girly-girl. Items that were pink and sparkly did not grab my attention. There were no posters of kitty cats neatly arranged in wicker baskets hanging on the walls of my blue bedroom. Phrases like, "That's so cute!" never came out of my mouth. Instead of crying during sappy movies, I made fun of their predictable plots. Coming from a home that rarely showed displays of affection, I hardly ever cried or got overly emotional, which I always thought was the mark of a "true girl" for some reason. So I often found myself wondering, *Am I doing this whole "girl thing" right?*

That thought stuck around into high school, and when I went to college, the question of how to do this "girl thing" took on a new twist. In college, the real awakening of my faith happened. As a theology major at a small, liberal arts institution, I was surrounded by faithful Catholic women who seemed to have this "girl thing" down. Consequently, I now had something new to wonder about as I began to ask myself, "Am I doing this whole *Catholic* girl thing right?" My curiosity was piqued as my miraculous-medal-wearing female friends discussed their deep devotion to Mary. *Do I love Mary enough?* I would wonder. *She's great and all, but I've never really thought of her as my affectionate* Mother ... *in fact, that seems super weird.* When I saw one of my friends tear up over an image of the pope kissing a baby, I thought, *Yup, I feel nothing ... isn't it normal not to cry over baby-loving popes, or am I missing something here?* As these women talked about how excited they were to get married and have enough kids to field a soccer team, all I could think was, *Is it OK if the idea of having a family who fills an entire pew at Mass kind of freaks me out?* When I added it all together, I was reasonably confident that I was doing something wrong when it came to Catholic womanhood.

Years later, when the invitation came for me to take the stage and explain to everyone how to be a Catholic woman, not much had changed with my feelings of inadequacy. I was now married with two small children, and the pressure to live up to the ideal of Catholic womanhood seemed to be stronger than ever. At the time, perhaps partly thanks to the rise of social media and mommy blogs, the image I had come up with for the perfect Catholic woman was a completely put together, Pinterest-worthy woman who balanced her vocation as wife, mother, and, for some, worker, with perfect ease and domesticity—all with a splash of creative liturgical living. So, chasing after that image, I tried to play the part. I made home-cooked meals for my family, I sewed saint costumes for my kids for Halloween–All Saints Day, and I kept a neat and orderly house. For the most part, I did enjoy doing many of these things, yet on the inside, I still felt like a fake.

Taking It On

Still feeling like I was not doing this whole "girl thing" right was where I found myself as I contemplated how to respond to that invitation for SEEK 2013. On the one hand, I felt incompetent; on the other, I saw an opportunity—an opportunity to dive deeply into a hidden question that had been in my heart for years: "What *does* it mean to be a woman?" If there was, in fact, something to this femininity thing, if there was a genuine uniqueness to womanhood, I wanted to know what it was.

I wanted to discover it because, as I saw it, there were plenty of identities in my life that I had taken on temporarily. Temporarily, I had been a student at a particular school, an employee of a certain company, a specific team or club member. But a woman? That was one thing in life that would not change. So, if I spent my time trying to understand something about myself, understanding my femininity seemed like a worthwhile undertaking.

It was for this reason that I said yes to giving the SEEK talk all those years ago. I knew I needed to understand my life as a woman better. I knew I needed to ask the hard questions that I had avoided out of my fear of their answers. (What if, according to the Church, the true mark of a woman is to cry when watching romantic comedies? I would be doomed.) I knew I needed to study, research, and pray through what the Church taught on this topic instead of drawing vague conclusions. I knew I needed to sit with my thoughts and findings for long enough to allow myself to internalize and make them my own.

The Journey

So, ladies, I come to you as a fellow sister on a journey of discovery. I still do not have it all figured out, and I do not think I ever will, but I have pored through Church documents and scholarly works on femininity. I have spent hours conversing with other women about their experiences of being a Catholic woman today. I have dug deeply into the lives of female saints to understand better how they lived their femininity in whatever time or place they found themselves. And I have even studied the topic in depth during more than one class as I have pursued my master's degree in theology at the Augustine Institute. This book is the fruit of these labors.

It is a book for any woman who is ready to explore *what* it means to be an authentic woman and discover *how* to be an authentic woman. It is a book for those who are tired of the secular rhetoric that tries to tell us how we should act and who we should be. It is a book for those who are ready to drink up the Church's wisdom and be inspired by the lives of female saints. It is a book for those who are ready to make peace with their femininity.

Just days after I returned home from giving my first talk ever on femininity titled "Real Womanhood," the idea for this book took root. That was nearly a decade ago, and I have been waiting for just the right moment to put pen to paper. I have been waiting for a prompting by the Holy Spirit, for a fire in my heart that says, "now!" That moment has arrived.

My prayers are with you, sister. May the Holy Spirit guide you through this book as you seek to understand more fully the woman God created you to be.

CHAPTER 1

Can I Get a Definition, Please?

I can still remember the phone call. "That's right, we're looking for a talk on authentic Catholic femininity," the SEEK conference coordinator's voice spoke in my ear. "You know, just highlights from Genesis and John Paul II." "Yeah, right. Of course," I responded, not wanting to sound like an idiot. "No problem. Just let me pray about it and I'll get back to you." I hung up the phone and dropped my head into my hands. *Why, God?* I thought.

Over the previous few years, the Lord had introduced an interesting side project into my life. Between raising babies, he slowly began opening up doors for me to speak at Catholic events. It was a fun outlet that fit my extroverted personality. After all, I had been voted "Most Likely to be a Motivational Speaker" by my fellow high school seniors. Recently I had spoken on a few college campuses about dating and given some talks for local mom's groups on liturgical living. But for all the reasons I have mentioned, the topic of Catholic womanhood felt way out of my wheelhouse. It would take some deep work to pull off, but I still said yes ... and then frantically began searching for answers.

Helper

I began my study in the book of Genesis, because that was one
of the few tips the event host left for me. It seemed like a natural
place to start. I already knew Genesis had some affirming things
to say about the creation of woman, when God made it clear that
both men and women were created in his image: "So God created
man in his own image, in the image of God he created him; male
and female he created them" (Genesis 1:27). I knew this was good
news because it meant that men and women are equal in their
worth, value, and dignity. Men are not better than women, and
women are not better than men. That part of Genesis was easy. It
was what came in chapter two that made me a bit nervous.

In the second creation account—which zooms in and looks at some
details surrounding God's creation of man and woman—Adam is
alone in the Garden. Seeing this as a problem, God declares, "It is not
good that the man should be alone; I will make him a helper fit for
him" (Genesis 2:18). God then creates a variety of potential helpers
for Adam's consideration. Because they are all animals, though, and
Adam is human, he cannot find a real connection with any of them;
he still feels alone. Understanding the dilemma, God puts Adam to
sleep, and from his rib, he creates another human, Eve. Upon waking,
Adam is relieved to see that this creation is finally his equal, as he
exclaims in verse 23: "This at last is bone of my bones, and flesh of my
flesh; she shall be called Woman, because she was taken out of Man."

What a sweet story, right? Adam was lonely. God made a helper fit
for him. Well ... let me tell you, when I comprehended this story in
middle school, I was none too pleased. I remember thinking, "Wait,
what? Did the Bible just say that God created Eve, who represents all
of us women, to be man's *helper*? Really!?" The idea made me think
of a little five-year-old girl whose worth needs to be validated, so her
mom calls her a "special helper" and gives her some unimportant,
menial job to do. *Helper? What a joke!* I thought.

Unfortunately, as an adult, I never quite got over my middle school anxiety regarding the implications of Genesis 2:18. Over the years, I did hear some theological thoughts about how the word helper is better translated as "helpmate" and how, as a helpmate, Eve had the privilege of serving alongside Adam. While these were not false statements, they really didn't help me feel any better. Simply calling it a privilege for women to be a helpmate seemed just as annoying. So, in a frantic search to figure out how to explain this, I turned my attention to the writings of the Church. Much to my surprise, the answer I had been looking for was right there in the wisdom of my favorite pope, St. John Paul II. During one of his weekly general audience addresses, he said,

> That woman is presented as a "helper fit for him" (Genesis 2:18) should not be interpreted as meaning that woman is man's servant—"helper" is not the equivalent of "servant" ... rather, the whole statement means that woman is able to collaborate with man because she complements him perfectly.[1]

Here was an answer I was looking for: Eve was never meant to be Adam's doormat. It was never God's intention for their relationship to be one of a master and a servant. This was the good news I assumed was out there, and now I had finally found the concrete evidence for it. My fears began to melt away as I continued my search and uncovered even more from John Paul II:

> The creation of woman is thus marked from the outset by the principle of help: a help which is not one-sided but mutual ... Womanhood and manhood are complementary ... It is only through the duality of the "masculine" and the "feminine" that the "human" finds full realization.[2]

---

1 John Paul II, General Audience (November 17, 1999), 1, vatican.va.

2 John Paul II, *Letter to Women* (June 29,1995), 7, vatican.va.

Being a helper was not just for Eve. My heart soared. Adam, too, was a helper, and it was from equal ground that they mutually helped each other in complementary ways.

Complementarity

Complementarity was another concept that I was familiar with from my studies on John Paul II's Theology of the Body, which is his series of teachings on human sexuality. However, I had somehow missed this key connection between it and Genesis. Like the word "complete," complementarity points toward *bringing things together* or *making something whole.* "Male" and "female" are two aspects of humanity—when one unifies them, "the 'human' finds full realization." In other words, the "human" gains a more complete understanding of who he or she is.

This abstract concept becomes visible in basic human biology when we consider how the male and female reproductive systems only make sense in light of each other. However, as I dove more deeply, I learned that biology is not the only place where the complementarity of men and women is displayed. In the abstract, men and women complement each other in their gifts and talents. They complement each other in how they lead, serve, and care for those entrusted to them.

Let me give an example of how this might work. Imagine that you are married to the love of your life, and you have two adorable young children. One night, while everyone is sound asleep, you awake to a loud commotion. Immediately it becomes clear that an intruder has broken into your house. What happens next?

I can tell you what would happen at my house. My husband, Kevin, would grab the most weapon-like object he could find to confront the intruder and do whatever it takes to protect our family. But what about me? What would I do?

First, let me tell you what I would *not* do. I would not pull my sheets up tight and plead to be saved like a damsel in distress. Nope. What I would do is run to the rooms of my babies, gather them as close as I could, and do whatever it takes to get them to safety.

Like my husband, I would go into protector mode; however, my protector mode would look a bit different from his. Rather than rush to confront the intruder, I would rush to my babies. Why might my husband and I instinctively act in similar but different ways? Because without having time to think, we would be operating from our complementary inclinations. Our thoughts would both be on protecting; however, we would be going about it in different ways that, when put together, would help protect our family.[3]

With complementarity afresh on my mind, my research took a new turn. If men and women have been created with complementary gifts that help each other, then I wanted to know: What exactly are these gifts that women possess, and what might they have to do with being an authentic Catholic woman?

The Feminine Genius

As my investigation continued, I discovered that in the late 1980s and '90s a marked emphasis on women emerged in the writings of St. John Paul II. He began dedicating weekly addresses, letters, and even encyclicals to the topic of the unique gifts that women bring to the world. In these exhortations he frequently spoke of these gifts in conjunction with the phrase the "genius of woman" or the "feminine genius." (If you are a history lover like me, check out the appendix for more on the origins of this powerful little phrase.)

---

3   This example came to me from Tony Brandt of Casting Nets. Shortly after his first daughter was born, he and his wife had this actual scenario play out in real life! And yes, he went to confront the bad guy while she guarded the baby.

This was a term I had heard before, but I had written it off. For whatever reason, telling a woman she was a "feminine genius" reminded me of cutesy phrases people tell little girls like: "You're God's little princess," or "You are so precious in his sight." Yes, I know, these statements are true, and little girls need to hear them, but they just never resonated with me. Telling a grown woman she was a "feminine genius" seemed like an adult version of telling girls they were princesses. It felt patronizing, as if people were still trying to convince women that despite their "weak femininity," they were still *special*.

Yet this was not at all what John Paul II was trying to do. As I read his works, I realized he knew the value of women. He understood their gifts were not secondary to those of men but vital in their own right. As he puts it, "Woman has a genius all her own, which is vitally essential to both society and the Church."[4]

While the Church had not been silent regarding women, St. John Paul II had an intentional reason for highlighting the gifts of women at this time in history. In the late 1980s and early '90s, a new trend was changing the way the world viewed femininity. Archetypal femininity was no longer seen as a strength but rather a weakness. The world declared that "true" women needed to toughen up like men if they wanted to prove themselves in male-dominated spheres. In fact, to be a woman meant that you asserted yourself like a man.

As a child of the 1980s, I certainly was affected by this shift and clearly remember being told as a little girl that anything a guy could do, I could do it better. Looking back, it was probably these cultural trends that pushed me to reject everything "girly," as I described in the introduction. While it is critical to encourage girls

---

4   John Paul II, "Angelus" (July 23, 1995), in *John Paul II Speaks on Women*, ed. Brooke Williams Deely (Washington, DC: Catholic University of America Press, 2014), para. 2.

to become confident women who know who they are, what was being propagated to me was a twisted girl power that translated to "be like a man power," and I bought it.

My whole community bought it. If you were to thumb through the photo albums of my childhood, mixed between photos of birthday parties and Christmases, you would find proof of this in some snapshots from Career Day circa 1992. There is my big sister standing in front of the fireplace, clutching a briefcase. Her slicked-back hair is in a tight bun, and she is wearing a business suit with extra thick shoulder pads. Why? Because she was a rising businesswoman and all businesswomen in the '80s and '90s put foam in their suit jackets to give them the appearance of broader shoulders to look more like men. (Incidentally, my mom must have had higher hopes for my sister that year than me. I stood next to her in her power suit with an apron and notepad— the tools of a waitress. To my mom's credit, I think she just did not want to go shopping for an outfit that fit whatever whim of a career I was leaning toward as a nine-year-old.)

So at a time when the world was saying, "Hey ladies, become like men," John Paul II emphatically responded by saying, "No, please ladies, do *not* try to become like men! What you have to offer to the world as women is unique, and your feminine gifts and strengths are desperately needed!" Of course, the pope put it more eloquently, but he was genuinely concerned about "some trends in the feminist movement" that "sought to make [woman] like man in every way."[5] He knew that if women failed to recognize the beauty of their feminine genius, then the world would be robbed of their distinct contributions.

As I processed John Paul II's words, I sadly realized that now, nearly twenty years later, many of his fears have come true.

---

5   John Paul II, General Audience (December 6, 1995), in *John Paul II Speaks on Women*, para. 1.

The defeminization of women had taken its toll, and in a variety of ways, the world I lived in was being robbed of the distinct contributions of women. I noticed that young adult women (myself included) often overlooked and ignored their uniqueness, not necessarily because they were rejecting it, but because they did not understand it or even know it existed. The worth of their femininity had not been fully passed on. As a result, they were feeling lost when it came to womanhood—and even, at times, life.

The new vision of femininity told them life is about living selfishly, finding pleasure, chasing dreams, and proving themselves. It told them that their life as a woman had no universal purpose, and so their goal was to define womanhood for themselves. How freeing, right? Yet, as I watched women aimlessly search to find *their* version of purpose, I noticed that they were not feeling fulfilled; instead, they were feeling empty and confused.

As I took it all in, I came to the realization that for a long time, the Church had been talking about a crisis of manhood, but now it was time to start talking about the *crisis of womanhood*. Women no longer knew or understood what it meant to be women. I didn't know, either ... but at least now I had somewhere to start as I considered John Paul II's feminine genius.

Can I Get a Definition, Please?

Interestingly, despite all of my digging, I never found St. John Paul II give a clear, concise definition of the genius of woman. I love clarity, so this fact was very frustrating at first, but the more I dive into the concept, the more I understand why.

First, the feminine genius is not a defined doctrine of the Church. One does not need to take a "black and white stance" on it as we must on doctrines such as the Trinity or the Incarnation—they must be accepted as a matter of faith. So the feminine genius will not be something you will see debated about and then given an official definition by the Church's Magisterium.

Second, the feminine genius is not just an *aspect* of being a woman but the *essence* of being a woman. Because there are so many angles from which we can look at the feminine genius, trying to pin it down to one sentence presents a challenge! So, without a word-for-word definition in the writings of John Paul II, we are left to do some ruminating over this concept.

But for Real, Though, Can I get a Definition, Please?

Though St. John Paul II never defined the feminine genius, it is important to have a framework to launch from when trying to understand this concept. For that definition, I find the brilliant work of Sister Prudence Allen, RSM, to be immensely helpful.

Sister Prudence, appointed by Pope Francis to serve on the International Theological Commission, is a philosopher of gender who has devoted several decades of her life to the study of womanhood. The fruit of her labors is a three-volume, more than two-thousand-page magnum opus entitled *The Concept of Woman*. Of all the definitions of the feminine genius, I find the one she shares in this work to be the most concise and helpful. Since Sister Prudence is a brilliant philosopher, even her "concise" definition can be a bit daunting. Fear not, though! After we present it, we will dive in to a deeper explanation.

According to Sister Prudence, "The phrase 'genius of woman' refers to a way of being, acting, and loving in the world, which manifests a unique creativity in human relationships. Women's acts of genius reveal a particular feminine sensitivity toward other human beings."[6]

---

6   Sister Prudence Allen, RSM, *The Concept of Woman: Volume III: The Search for Communion of Persons, 1500–2015* (Grand Rapids, MI: William B. Eerdmans Publishing Company, 2016), 475.

To start, Sister Prudence is talking about "a way of being." As we have seen, this means that the genius of woman is not an *aspect* of femininity; rather, it is the very *essence* of it. It has to do with who women are, how they act, and how they love—in sum, the nature of womanhood.

Second, the definition talks about "creativity in human relationships." So the feminine genius is not about intellectual knowledge or practical skills but the distinctive way women approach others.

Finally, Sister Prudence concludes that a woman's "acts of genius"—that is, *how a woman puts her genius into the world*— show "a particular feminine sensitivity toward other human beings." When a woman lives from her feminine genius, then, her actions show that she has a unique way of seeing people.

St. John Paul II often writes of this "feminine sensitivity toward other human beings." In his *Letter to Women*, he summarizes it in this way: "Perhaps more than men, women *acknowledge the person*, because they see persons with their hearts. They see them independently of various ideological or political systems. They see others in their greatness and limitations."[7] Basically, women are especially gifted in their ability to see people as people, not objects or things. (More on this later.)

So, in an attempt to bring this together in a simple way, think of the feminine genius as the *person-oriented disposition* of woman. It is the unique, feminine way women relate to humanity.

Feminine Genius Gifts

While St. John Paul II never defines the feminine genius, he does highlight gifts that flow from a woman's feminine genius. As I reviewed his works on women, these gifts began to surface, and I created a list of the ones he seemed to focus on the most.

---

7   John Paul II, *Letter to Women*, 12.

If you have ever seen a definition of the feminine genius before in a non-academic presentation, it likely included something about the unique gifts and contributions that women bring to the world. While a woman's gifts are related to the feminine genius, I would not say that having "feminine gifts" is the definition of the feminine genius. Rather, a woman's complementary gifts are the fruit—the result of—her feminine genius. A woman has a tendency to possess and display particular feminine gifts *because of* her feminine genius.

Concentrating on these gifts that John Paul II seemed to reference the most as he talked about women gave me clues into his thoughts on the various aspects of a woman's unique, person-oriented genius and how women distinctively contribute to the world. Soon, understanding and exploring how to live from my list of gifts became my focus—and the backbone for the rest of this book.

Before giving my list, please note that these words are not an official, Vatican-approved list—a list like that does not exist. There are varying lists of "feminine genius gifts" that will turn up on a Google search, and these offer many helpful insights into women's nature. Yet it is important to note that St. John Paul II never presents us with a list of feminine genius words, aspects, charisms, gifts, or values. Any list is simply an interpretation of the pope's work.

So, rather than claim that what I am sharing is *the* decisive list associated with the feminine genius, these are simply eight words that I frequently see in John Paul II's writing on women. In combing his works, I have done my best to come up with a foundational list of gifts, but I do not claim that it is a definitive one.

Eight Feminine Gifts

Now that we have had a sufficient build-up, without further ado, here are the eight feminine gifts I have identified.

- ♥ Self-giving

- ♥ Receptivity

- ♥ Maternity

- ♥ Sensitivity

- ♥ Intuition

- ♥ Generosity

- ♥ Fidelity

- ♥ Strength

Each of these words describes a quality, attribute, charism, or value that St. John Paul II spoke or wrote about in conjunction with what women bring to the world in a unique and privileged way. In this book, I will be using the word "gifts" to describe these contributions of women because that is the word John Paul II himself used most often.

Keep in mind that these gifts are not the *only* gifts that women possess. If you look at the list and feel like something is missing, that is because it is. Summing up the vast gifts women bring to the world is impossible. Each woman is unique, and her gifts cannot be boxed into just eight words. However, to chase after what John Paul II praised and pondered, I will focus on these eight.

Now before you roll your eyes and write this off as just another way to promote feminine stereotypes, first hear me out because these words are not meant to be stereotypes.

Stereotypical versus Typical

Nobody likes to be stereotyped. There is something about the way stereotypes box us in that can leave us feeling misunderstood. Statements like, "All women _____," or "There are no females who can _____," leave us feeling pigeonholed into a description that we might not identify with. Stereotypes create such a response because they take what is *typical* of a group and exaggerate it to a skewed extreme.

This is not at all what John Paul II is trying to do when he highlights a typical gift that he finds in women. For example, when he says that women have a unique sensitivity, he is not saying that all women are blubbering balls of irrational emotion who cannot be trusted ... especially at certain times of the month. No. This is a stereotypical view of sensitivity that our culture has created and put a box around. Rather, John Paul II highlights the gift of sensitivity to praise women for contributing to the world a unique awareness of others' needs.

Furthermore, he does not expect every woman to manifest these gifts in exactly the same way. It is important to note here that just because there are common, or typical, traits among all women, this does not mean that there is only one way for all women to express that trait. Within the realm of "typical," there is room for every gift to be expressed in a variety of individual ways.

Out of necessity, when taking deep dives into these gifts, we will be looking at broad strokes. However, as we move along, look for ways to express each feminine genius gift in your unique way, which is wonderful and only adds to the Church's beauty.

Finally, if you are looking at this list and feeling like there are particular gifts that you do not relate to, this does not mean you are not a woman. There was a time in my life when a few of these gifts were not words I would use to describe myself, and there are still certain ones that I feel more connected to than others. If this is true for you, all I can ask for at this point is your trust. A goal of this book is to break open these gifts in a new way, which will allow you to think about them from a new angle and help you to see how past experiences and influences may be keeping you from understanding them.

Deep Dives

The foundation has been laid. Now it is time to take a deep dive into each of the eight complementary gifts, qualities, attributes, charisms, or values that St. John Paul II highlights when he speaks about the feminine genius. Moving forward, each chapter will explore one of the gifts of the feminine genius in depth.

As you will see, there is a specific plan for each feminine genius deep dive:

1. The gift will be introduced, and then we will look at what John Paul II has to say about it.

2. There will be a story of a woman, or group of women, who have revealed this gift in an exemplary way.

3. We will explore how the gift can become twisted into a weakness, followed by practical thoughts on preventing that from happening.

4. A challenge will be offered for how we could put this gift into practice.

While this is certainly a book you could read straight through, I suggest that you slow down and read one chapter at a time. This book is intended to help you grow in your feminine genius gifts, and this requires some processing. So allow yourself the time to digest each chapter and consider its challenge before moving on to the next gift.

Finally, while all women share a common nature, each woman will express this nature in her own way. As you read, keep in mind that there will be varying degrees to which you identify with some of these gifts, as there is always an inherent danger when we speak in generalities. If you do not connect with a specific gift, this just means that how you express a particular gift might not resonate with the angle from which it is being presented. I have tried to sum them up using universal experiences, but it is impossible to capture every aspect of a particular gift. So I encourage you to internalize and process this content looking for how it applies to *you*—in all your unique glory and perfection.

Are you ready? It is time to move forward and take on the challenge that St. John Paul II gives us in his *Letter to Women*:

> It is thus my hope, dear sisters, that you will reflect carefully on what it means to speak of the *"genius of women,"* not only in order to be able to see in this phrase a specific part of God's plan which needs to be accepted and appreciated, but also in order to let this genius be more fully expressed in the life of society as a whole, as well as in the life of the Church.[8]

---

8   John Paul II, 10.

Discussion Questions

1. What impressions have the creation stories in the Bible given you?

2. Has your understanding of their meaning changed over time? How?

3. What are some ways that you have seen complementarity lived out in your own experiences?

4. Have you heard of the *feminine genius*? If not, what do you think of this term? If you were familiar with the feminine genius before reading about it here, what was your understanding of it? Has your understanding changed in any way as a result of what you read?

5. Of the list of feminine genius gifts presented—self-giving, receptivity, maternity, sensitivity, intuition, generosity, fidelity, and strength—which do you identify with the most? Why? Which gifts do you identify with the least? Why?

6. In what ways have stereotypes about femininity and masculinity affected how you see yourself and others?

CHAPTER 2

Self-Giving and St. Edith Stein

As a child, I loved to imagine what heaven looked like. While trying to fall asleep, I would picture a cloud-filled landscape with children floating everywhere. On one side were seesaws and swings that somehow grounded themselves in white fluff. On the other was a large kickball field, and everyone playing was having a great time. Basically, my idea of heaven was recess—with the exception of a cloud staircase that divided the two play areas. At the top was an old man with a white beard (God, of course) who sat on his throne and happily watched everyone play.

From a young age, I knew that my faith taught that God made humans in his image and likeness. I assumed this meant that God looked a lot like me—except he was really old from having been around for eternity. Later in life, I was somewhat disappointed to learn that my theology was more than a bit off.

Image and Likeness

To say humans are created in God's image and likeness does not mean that we look like God or that God looks like us. Instead, it means that there are certain ways our being reflects God's being. For example, humans have an intellect, which means we can reason; and humans have free will, which means we can choose.

With the exception of the angels, nothing else in God's creation can do these two things. Another way humanity reflects, or images, our Creator is in our capacity to give of ourselves to others, in a way that reflects the life of the Trinity.

The Trinity is a communion of divine Persons, whose love continuously pours out from one Person to another. God the Father pours out his very being of love to God the Son, and in turn, God the Son pours out his very being of love to God the Father. The self-giving love that pours out between them is the Holy Spirit.

For St. John Paul II, imaging this self-giving love of the Trinity is fundamental to humanity's discovery of who God has created us to be. Time and again, John Paul II quotes a famous line from the Second Vatican Council document *Gaudium et spes*: "Man cannot fully find himself except through a sincere gift of himself."[9] This is probably one of the most famous lines from that council, and perhaps the sentence John Paul II quoted more than any other. It means that if men and women genuinely want to discover who they are, if they want to discover their purpose and vocation, they can only do so by giving themselves in service to and out of love for others. To put it another way, humans can only discover who they are in relation to those around them, and they can only discover those around them by giving themselves to others.

Ever reminding people of their call to give of themselves, at the beginning of his *Letter to Women*—written for the 1995 United Nations conference on women—John Paul II shares his hope for the event:

> Necessary emphasis should be placed on the *"genius of women,"* not only by considering great and famous women of the past or present, but also those *ordinary* women who reveal the gift of their womanhood by placing themselves at the service of others in their everyday lives. For in giving themselves to others each day women fulfill their deepest vocation.[10]

---

9   Second Vatican Council, *Gaudium et spes* (December 7, 1965), 24, vatican.va.

10   John Paul II, *Letter to Women*, 12.

By reflecting the Trinity and giving of themselves to others, women fulfill their deepest calling.

Human Gifts

You may have noticed that this first "feminine genius gift" is not exclusive to women. This is because self-giving is just as much a call for men as it is for women. In fact, God calls all human beings, men and women, to live each of the gifts explored in this book in complementary ways. These gifts, or "values," as Pope Benedict XVI calls them, are not just feminine genius gifts; they are "above all human values."[11]

When St. John Paul II was pope, Joseph Cardinal Ratzinger (the future Pope Benedict XVI) was the prefect for the Congregation for the Doctrine of the Faith. During this time, Cardinal Ratzinger wrote a letter for the Church entitled *On the Collaboration of Men and Women in the Church and in the World*. Here, he comments beautifully on a woman's "capacity for the other,"[12] which is her ability to selflessly live for others. After conveying some of the gifts that are connected to this ability, he clarifies that these values are not restricted to women:

> It is appropriate however to recall that the feminine values mentioned here are above all human values ... It is only because women are more immediately attuned to these values that they are the reminder and the privileged sign of such values. But, in the final analysis, every human being, man or woman, is destined to be "for the other."[13]

Here, Benedict is affirming that feminine gifts, or values, are for

---

11   Joseph Cardinal Ratzinger and Angelo Amato, *Letter to the Bishops of the Catholic Church on the Collaboration of Men and Women in the Church and in the World* (May 31, 2004), 14, vatican.va.

12   Ratzinger and Amato, 13.

13   Ratzinger and Amato, 14.

both genders. However, because "women are more immediately attuned" to these gifts, and to living "for the other," they are the "privileged sign," or example, of these things. Therefore, it is woman's responsibility to bring these person-oriented gifts into the world and model them to the men in their life, *who are also called to cultivate and express these gifts in their own, complementary, masculine way.*

When it comes to self-giving, the example of pregnancy is a straightforward way that women uniquely give themselves to others. Through offering up their entire body for the sake of another, women show a literal "capacity for the other." Even after birth, this self-giving does not end as a mother continues to give her time, love, emotions, and resources to her growing child. However, pregnancy and motherhood are not the only ways women uniquely reveal self-giving in this world. One woman who beautifully demonstrates this is St. Teresa Benedicta of the Cross, or Edith Stein.

Meet St. Edith Stein

In 1891, Edith Stein was born on the holiest day in the Jewish year, Yom Kippur, the Day of Atonement. Her devout Jewish family lived in what is now Wroclaw, Poland, which, at the time, was part of the German Empire. Edith, the youngest of eleven children, grew up in a home that encouraged education and critical thinking. Despite her admiration for her mother's deep faith, she became a professed atheist by her teens.

Although she rejected God, Edith still had a profound desire for truth and goodness, which led her to study for a doctorate in philosophy. Intellectual pursuits were not her only love, however, as she had a profound love for humanity. When World War I broke out, Edith, who was in her twenties, took a year-long break from her studies to tend to the sick as a volunteer wartime Red Cross nurse in an infectious disease hospital.

After the war, Edith finished her doctoral dissertation, entitled *On the Problem of Empathy*, and she began teaching at the University of Freiburg in Germany. As you might expect, her stance as a woman in higher education, who taught philosophy of all things, was not always well-received or respected. Despite her brilliant mind, she was unable to advance in her career due to her gender. In the end, though, Edith's place was not in higher education. God had other plans for her.

While on summer break in 1921, Edith read St. Teresa of Avila's autobiography, and a conversion to Christ quickly began to take root in her heart. Just months later, on January 1, 1922, she was baptized into the Catholic Church. With her newfound faith, Edith began teaching at a Dominican school, and her philosophical writings began incorporating the Catholic Faith. These changes led her to become a lecturer at the Catholic Institute for Scientific Pedagogy. However, due to her Jewish ethnicity, in 1933, she was forced by the Nazi authorities to abandon her teaching position. Around this time, nearly a decade after she became a Catholic, Edith answered a call to become a discalced Carmelite nun.

Shortly after she took her final vows in 1938, the Nazi reign of terror on anyone of Jewish heritage had stepped into high gear. Her Carmelite superiors recognized the danger, so they transferred Edith, now Sister Teresa Benedicta of the Cross, and her sister Rose, who was a Third Order Carmelite, to a monastery in Echt, Netherlands. Upon arriving, Sister Teresa continued her vocation as a philosophy teacher; however, she knew in her heart that her life would one day end in a concentration camp. As a result of this intuition, she wrote a will and began training herself for life in captivity by enduring the cold and allowing herself to feel hunger. Rather than run from her perceived fate, she welcomed it. As time would tell, Sister Teresa's intuition proved correct.

In July of 1942, the bishops' conference of the Netherlands publicly condemned the racist persecution of the Nazis, and they retaliated by ordering the arrest of all Jewish converts to the Catholic Faith. Days later, Sister Teresa and Rose were arrested and began their journey to Auschwitz. A week after their arrival, Sister Teresa and Rose were presumably taken to a small, boarded-up farmhouse just outside the camp and died along with many others by poison gas.

Revealing the Gift of Self-Giving

For those familiar with Edith Stein's story and writings, it can be easy to see her as an intellectual with whom it would be awkward to share a cup of coffee. But those who were close to Edith knew that, behind her brilliant mind, was a caring and thoughtful woman who cherished everyone, especially her students. Among the thousands of pages written by Edith, one of my favorites is not one of her *Essays on Woman* or an article on phenomenology. It is a simple letter she wrote to one of her former students, Anneliese Lichtenberger.

In 1931, Anneliese wrote to Edith to seek her counsel in a disappointing situation. She had recently been placed on academic probation and feared that she would not be able to pull her grades up before the end of the term. No doubt Edith read her letter with a saddened heart, and she responded warmly by asking her, "Among the books you got as a child, do you have Andersen's Fairy Tales? If so, read the story of the ugly duckling. I believe in your swan-destiny."[14]

I believe in your swan-destiny. Few responses from a teacher to a student could be more tender.

Edith went on in the letter and further advised Anneliese, "Don't hold it against others if they haven't discovered this yet, and don't let yourself become bitter. You are not the only one to make

---

14   Edith Stein, *Self Portrait in Letters: 1916–1942*, ed. L. Gelber and Romaeus Leuven, trans. Josephine Koeppel (Washington, DC: ISC Publications, 1993), 101.

mistakes day after day—we all do it. But the Lord is patient and full of mercy. In his household of grace he can use our faults, too, if we lay them on the altar for him."[15]

This is the often-overlooked side of Edith that I love so dearly, the side where she gave of herself to the world in so many ways. As a nurse and as a teacher, she cared for and nurtured each soul left in her charge. As a philosopher, she gave of her intellect to the world. As a martyr, she gave of herself in the ultimate way by offering her life for the Church.

It would have been easy for Edith to resent the Dutch bishops' choice to speak out against the Nazis. After all, if they had remained silent, she may have survived the Holocaust. But Edith did not resent their choice to condemn Nazism, because the opportunity to give her life for the body of Christ, the Church, was something she welcomed. Remarkably, on June 6, 1939, two years before her death, she wrote:

> I joyfully accept in advance the death God has appointed for me, in perfect submission to his most holy will. May the Lord accept my life and death for the honor and glory of his name, for the needs of his holy Church—especially for the preservation, sanctification, and final perfecting of our holy Order, and in particular for the Carmels of Cologne and Echt—for the Jewish people, that the Lord may be received by his own and his Kingdom come in glory, for the deliverance of Germany and peace throughout the world, and finally for all my relatives living and dead and all whom God has given me: many none of them be lost.[16]

Edith was not afraid of giving herself, sacrificing herself, in atonement for the sins of the world. She wanted to die so that she could mystically give herself for the conversion of the world. For the woman born on

---

15 Stein, 101.

16 Waltraud Herbstrith, *Edith Stein: The Untold Story of the Philosopher and Mystic Who Lost Her Life in the Death Camps of Auschwitz*, trans. Bernard Bonowitz (San Francisco: Ignatius Press, 1985), 168–169.

the Jewish Feast of Atonement, her martyrdom was a providential life's bookend that no one could have predicted.

How Can Self-Giving Get Twisted?

In my life, I have noticed that sometimes my greatest strengths can become my greatest weaknesses. I can sometimes take the gifts that God has given me and allow them to become twisted, and they end up working against me. This is true of all the gifts of the feminine genius, and I know that I am not the only woman who has experienced this reality. So, after exploring each gift, I will examine a weakness that can twist that gift and then suggest ways to face it.

As St. Edith Stein's life demonstrates, women have a unique ability to give themselves to others, making it natural for us to want to be there for others. Being helpful is who we are. Giving to others is what we do. However, in our desire to give, we can sometimes find ourselves in situations where life becomes overwhelming. In those moments, the idea that self-giving leads to happiness can feel like a joke.

As my Catholic Faith teaches, I know that the only way to find myself is by losing myself. But from a fallen human perspective, many times I have thrown my hands up and said, "It's not working! I'm giving and giving, but I don't feel fulfilled. I just feel exhausted!"

Of course, I love my husband, but I do not always feel like I have the energy to be the wife he deserves. Of course, I love my four spectacular children, but they have so many needs. Of course, I love my apostolate, and I know I am called to it, but, wow, does it require a lot of headspace and planning. Each of these things is so important, so I give. And I give. And I give. And sometimes I love it. But sometimes—like a child doing everything she can to delay bedtime—all I want to do is get to my to-do list so I can feel like I accomplished something that day. In those moments, I am not finding myself as I struggle to give of myself to others patiently. You have been there, right? Surely, you know what I am talking about. The truth is that selfless giving does not come naturally in our broken world. Yet the fact remains that "in giving [them] selves to others each day women fulfill their deepest vocation."[17]

What Can We Do About It?

The basic solution to the "running-on-empty" problem is a buzzword that lives strong in the hashtag world: self-care. While it is a start to fixing the problem, it is a risky one to put forward because it can take two extremes that render it useless.

On the one hand, sometimes we feel guilty taking time for ourselves and never actually do it. This is especially true during busy seasons, such as working on a deadline, preparing for holidays, planning a wedding, studying for finals, or welcoming a new baby. In these moments, it seems like the last thing we have time for is ourself.

The problem with this approach is that if we do not take care of ourselves, we risk burnout. Giving until it hurts is a beautiful thing, yet at the same time, each of us is a real human being with real needs. Making sure we meet those legitimate needs is not wimpy; actually, it is smart.

On the other hand, some of us are tempted to use the self-care banner as a way to justify vices. Eating a dessert after every meal because the package says, "You deserve it!"? Self-care. Staying up until midnight to binge-watch the latest drama series? Self-care. Buying stuff you do not need because it feels good at the moment? Self-care.

---

17   John Paul II, 12.

I know these examples well because I have used them. But there is a fundamental problem when using these types of excuses: deep down, we all know that binge-watching, excessively eating sweets, or therapy shopping are not self-care. They can actually be quite the opposite—bad habits that ultimately leave us feeling drained and empty.

The key to finding the self-care balance is understanding a straightforward truth: Self-care is not about you; it is about others. It is about taking care of yourself, *so you can live your deepest vocation of reflecting the Trinity through self-giving love.*

Five Categories

There are a staggering number of resources available on self-care, with each program claiming to have found the right formula for finding peace and balance. For this reason, I am not going to pretend like I have the magic solution here, but I do want to propose five simple categories for you to consider when it comes to self-care that supports self-giving.

1. *Sleep.* When I am feeling overwhelmed, my spiritual director asks me if I am getting enough sleep. She asks because she knows that sleep is essential for self-giving. The right amount each person needs can vary, but I urge you to find the amount you need and do what you can to guard your sleep. And, please, skip the late-night screen time; you will never regret it.

   Perhaps the idea of a good night's sleep sounds wimpy compared to the life of an intense giver like St. Edith Stein, but she understood the importance of taking care of herself. In her *Essays on Woman*, she suggests that everyone take an afternoon break "to shed all cares *[sic]* for a short time before the tabernacle." She adds, "Whoever also possibly requires bodily rest, should take a breathing space in her own room."[18] Did you catch that? Edith says if you need a nap, take it!

2. *Nutrition.* Skipping meals to prep for an important meeting or eating toddler scraps and calling it lunch will leave you struggling for the energy you need. Our bodies need fuel to live selflessly. Regular, nutritious meals and plenty of water can go a long way in keeping you sane.

3. *Exercise.* Get your body moving! Whether you hit the gym for an intense cardio class followed by weight training or you go on a walk after dinner, get your exercise every single day.

4. *Leisure.* Leisure time does not mean mindlessly zoning out, which is simply taking a break, at best. Authentic leisure is participating in activities that make you come alive. Spending time in community, having real conversations, doing a hobby you love with no agenda, getting into nature, reading a favorite book, cooking a good meal, creating with your hands—all of these activities are true leisure.

Any day of the week can be appropriate for leisure, but setting aside Sundays for nothing but prayer and leisure is a foolproof way to rejuvenate for the week ahead. Knowing this secret, Edith wrote, "Sunday must be a great door through which celestial life can enter into everyday life, and strength for the work of the entire week."[19]

---

18 Edith Stein, *Essays on Woman,* trans. Freda Mary Oben, PhD (Washington, DC: ISC Publications, 2017), 144.

19 Stein, 145.

5. ***Prayer.*** This is hands down the most essential self-care category. Prayer is vital because without prayer, there is nothing. Perhaps you have some firsthand experience with this, yet still, when things get busy, prayer can easily be the first thing to go.

    St. Teresa of Calcutta's Missionaries of Charity once came to her exhausted and overwhelmed. There were too many people to serve and not enough time to serve them. They asked her to rearrange their schedule to allow for more time for work. Do you know what she did? She cut back their daily work hours and added in another holy hour for prayer with the Lord.

    When things get busy, prayer is needed more than ever. For this reason, Edith suggested that prayer not be left to chance. Placing it as the first item on your daily agenda ensures that your day gets off on the right foot. Edith describes it this way:

    > The duties and cares of the day crowd about us when we awake in the morning (if they have not already dispelled our night's rest). How can all this be accommodated in one day? When will I do this, when that? How shall I start on this and that? Thus agitated, we would like to run around and rush forth. We must take the reins in hand and say "Take it easy! Not any of this may touch me now. My first mornings hour belongs to the Lord. I will tackle the day's work which he charges me with, and he will give me the power to accomplish it." [20]

    I know committing to daily prayer can seem impossible at times, but daily prayer is actually not complicated. I

---

20   Stein, 143.

have found that many people think they need a grand plan with multiple steps to obtain holiness, which makes them feel overwhelmed. But a grand plan is not what we need. The most important thing for prayer is just to show up no matter what.

When you are tired, show up. When you do not have time, show up. When you feel like prayer is dry, show up. Show up, saying, "Here I am, Lord," and take a deep breath. Read the Bible, utilize meditation books, pray the Rosary—whatever aids you in your daily conversation with God. Do not get lost in the weeds when it comes to prayer. Simply schedule a time and show up.

Self-Giving Challenge

For our first challenge, I invite you to develop a plan for taking care of your basic needs so that you do not end up running on empty. Using the five simple categories of sleep, nutrition, exercise, leisure, and prayer, come up with a reasonable and doable plan to make them each a priority.

Keep in mind that no matter how basic your plan is, you will not always execute it with one hundred percent accuracy. Do not let that discourage you. The point of your plan is not to give you a rigid checklist that leaves you feeling guilty when you fail at keeping it perfectly. The point is to provide you with something to aim for. Even if you do not hit all of it every time, you will hit some of it most of the time. And that is better than nothing. So get out a pen and paper and start planning how you will take care of you so you can take care of others.

Discussion Questions

1. Can you identify with the gift of self-giving? Why or why not? What factors in your life have either stifled or encouraged growth in this gift?

2. This chapter started with explaining how humans are called to image the Trinity through self-giving love. How does this affect the way you see God?

3. What did you find most inspiring about the life of St. Edith Stein? What lessons on feminine self-giving can you learn from her?

4. Which of the two self-care extremes do you more easily fall into—feeling guilty for taking time for yourself or using self-care as an excuse for vices?

5. On your self-care plan, which categories do you already succeed at? Which categories do you struggle with?

6. What is one way you can reveal the gift of self-giving to your family, friends, community, or world?

CHAPTER 3

Receptivity and Servant of God Chiara Corbella Petrillo

"We have only five loaves here and two fish," the apostles reported to Jesus, confusion in their voices. Unfazed by their concern, Jesus confidently responds, "Bring them here to me" (Matthew 14:17-18). Taking the loaves and fishes into his hands, he gave thanks, broke the bread, and gave the food back to the disciples with the instructions to go feed the people.

Can you imagine being a disciple of Jesus at that moment? The Lord hands you a small basket of food and tells you to feed five thousand men, plus an *untold number of women and children.* "How?" you wonder. "This basket of food will run out before even a small fraction of the crowd has been fed." Still, you obey and distribute what he has given to you. When you return to ask what to do next, Jesus refills your basket and tells you to go feed the people. Confused by the new abundance, you obey, give out the food, and return to Jesus. Again, he has more ... and more ... and more. Every time you run out, *Jesus always has more when you come back to him.*

The Secret Is Jesus

The previous chapter explored the gift of self-giving and offered self-care as a way to help prevent burnout. The first four self-care categories—sleep, nutrition, exercise, and leisure—addressed human needs. These needs are *real* needs and must be considered in times of struggle. However, nobody will find that the secret to living selflessly with joy is a balanced diet, rejuvenating vacation, or fulfilling hobby. The secret is Jesus.

To live selflessly, we have to recognize that we cannot do it on your own. The strength comes from God. It is only by receiving what we need from him that we can, in turn, give it to others. This is the lesson the disciples learned at the feeding of the five thousand, and it is a lesson for us today. Without God, there is nothing to give, but with him we have everything we need.

The key to living selflessly lies in being receptive to the help, or grace, that God wants to give to us. He always supplies us with what we need to live the life he has called us to, but he does not force us to accept it; we have to receive it willingly. For us women, this is good news because receptivity is a part of our very nature.

Written on Our Souls

In his theology of the body, St. John Paul II wrote extensively on how the male and female bodies are a "visible sign of an invisible reality."[21] In the marital embrace, or sex, a man's body is made to give, or initiate, and a woman's body is made to receive. This is just basic biology. Yet humans are more than just a body; we also have a soul. So deeply integrated is our body–soul composite that the soul and body reflect each other. Not only is man's body made to give in the marital embrace, but his soul is also made to give in

---

21 John Paul II, General Audience (July 28, 1982), in *John Paul II Speaks on Women*, para. 5.

the world. Likewise, not only is woman's body made to receive, or be receptive, in the marital embrace, but her soul is also made to receive, or be receptive, in the world. Woman's receptive nature is fundamental to the feminine genius, and, in many ways, it is the foundation of her feminine nature.

Before moving on, please note that receptivity is *not* passivity or inaction. Being receptive actually is quite the opposite. Being receptive is taking gifts and blessings presented to you and responding to them with love. For example, when you receive others into your home, it requires care and attention to ensure that they are welcomed and comfortable. Or if someone comes to you with a problem, you receive the person into your heart and give attention to his or her emotional or spiritual needs. Or when a woman's husband gives of himself in the marital embrace, the woman receives that gift and responds to it with love. None of these examples allow inaction; rather, they require a thoughtful and active response.

The same is true in the spiritual life. The Lord is always presenting what he desires to give us, but it is up to us to determine if we will actively accept his gifts and respond with our own gift of love, or if we will reject his gifts and respond with distrust. When we can accept and respond with love, we are fully reflecting the mutual pouring out of love seen in the Trinity. For this reason, what separates a peaceful heart from an agitated one is the ability to *accept all that God desires to give us and respond with a mutual gift of love.* Actively trusting that God is working all things for our good leads to peace because, when we live from this place, anything the Lord presents can be received as a gift.

A woman who lives the feminine genius gift of receptivity places her trust in God in all circumstances, like Servant of God Chiara Corbella Petrillo.

Meet Servant of God Chiara Corbella Petrillo

In June of 2013, I received emails from two friends who had recently encountered an extraordinary woman's story while in Rome. These women did not even know each other, but they both told me, "Lisa, you have got to hear this story of Chiara Corbella Petrillo—and share it!" I received these emails just days after this holy woman's funeral, but she is now *Servant of God* Chiara Corbella Petrillo, the first step toward possible canonization to sainthood in the Church.

Heeding my friends' advice, I shared Chiara's story a few months later at the SEEK 2013 conference, and have continued to share it since. To say that Chiara is close to my heart would be an understatement. Before I came to know her story, I thought holiness worthy of sainthood was just for those who founded religious orders, levitated, or were popes. Chiara's life included none of these things. Instead, her life looked a lot like mine—in fact, we were born just a few months apart. For me, Chiara made being a saint in our world today seem possible, and her life is the inspiration for why I am constantly telling people, "Be a saint. It's worth it!" I pray that her story inspires you as much as it has inspired me.

Saints Are Still Being Made

Servant of God Chiara Corbella Petrillo was born in Rome, Italy, in 1984. Her father worked in the tourist industry, which allowed her family to travel extensively. So, while on pilgrimage in the summer of 2002, she met her future husband, Enrico. Their path to marriage was a modern love story filled with fears, doubts, and periodic breakups, but eventually, they determined that there was no one else to whom they wanted to commit their lives.

A month after marrying in 2008, Chiara and Enrico conceived their first child. However, their joyous news was soon followed by complications when they learned that their baby had a rare condition that would make life outside of the womb impossible. Doctors offered Chiara the option to abort her daughter, but she declined. With heroic courage, she accepted the heartbreak of knowing her unborn child would not live long and chose to do whatever she could to give her child as much life as possible. Chiara carried baby Maria to term, and she was born and baptized. About half an hour later, she returned to the hands of her Father in heaven.

For a second time, Chiara became pregnant, and for a second time, complications arose as doctors determined that her baby boy would be born with many disabilities. Having already lost one child, Chiara and Enrico were undeterred and accepted their new child as a gift. However, they soon learned the prognosis was worse than initially supposed, and life outside of the womb would not be possible for this child either. Again, doctors offered Chiara the option to abort her baby, but again she chose to do whatever she could to give her son as much life as possible. Just as she did with baby Maria, Chiara carried baby Davide to term, and he was born and baptized. About half an hour later, like his sister, he returned to the hands of his Father in heaven.

After two intense experiences like this, nobody would blame Chiara if her heart became a bit hard and she no longer wanted to be receptive to new life. However, rather than closing in on herself, she spoke publicly about the blessings of her two children in heaven, and she remained open to life. She soon became pregnant a third time.

Given her first two pregnancies, Chiara's doctors monitored her closely and rejoiced with her as this pregnancy progressed smoothly. However, a new fear arose that nobody could have prepared for. A concerning tumor was growing on Chiara's tongue. Immediately, she underwent a painful surgery to remove the lesion, but it was found to be cancerous.

This news left Chiara with a harrowing decision. She needed to begin aggressive treatments to rid her body of cancer. But undergoing these treatments while pregnant would harm her unborn child, which for Chiara was not an option. The only other opportunity to protect her own life was to deliver her son, Francesco, prematurely and hope for the best. For Chiara, this was not a real option either.

She writes, "To a majority of the doctors, Francesco is a seven-month fetus. And the one who should be saved is me. But I have no intention of putting the life of Francesco at risk ... The difficult decision was to understand how to attack this tumor as soon as possible without putting the life of Francesco in peril." [22]

Chiara stood her ground to protect her son, and her doctor put together an alternative treatment plan. Soon after, in May 2011, baby Francesco was born healthy at thirty-seven weeks. A few days after giving birth, Chiara underwent another painful surgery, which revealed that her cancer had spread. Chemotherapy, radiation, and a host of other treatments followed, but, despite each effort, the cancer could not be stopped. By late March 2012, the disease was detected in Chiara's lungs, eye, liver, and breast. By April, her condition was declared terminal. Enrico heard the prognosis first, and her doctor thought it was best to have him tell Chiara. Her biography, written by two of her closest friends, recounts the moving scene:

> Enrico entered [Chiara's hospital room] and, holding back tears, called his wife. Enrico accompanied her to the hospital chapel, where he told her everything without saying anything. They embraced before the Lord and repeated their marriage vows. Out of fear that the devil might tempt her, she asked specifically: "Just do not tell me how much time remains, because I wish to live in the present." [23]

---

22 Simone Troisi and Cristiana Paccini, *Chiara Corbella Petrillo: A Witness to Joy*, trans. Charlotte J. Fasi (Manchester, NH: Sophia Institute Press, 2015), 85.

23 Troisi and Paccini, 120.

By June 13, Chiara's final day on earth arrived. From a wheelchair, she sat with Enrico gazing at Jesus in the tabernacle in her room. A question had been weighing on Enrico's heart, and at this moment, he finally found the courage to ask it. Thinking of Jesus' promise that his yoke is easy and his burden light (see Matthew 11:30), he asked, "Chiara, is this yoke, this cross, really sweet as Jesus said?"[24] Chiara turned her attention from the tabernacle to her husband and smiled. Weakly she replied, "Yes, Enrico, it is very sweet."[25]

Hours later, just like her children Maria and Davide, Chiara returned to the hands of her Father in heaven.

Revealing the Gift of Receptivity

To the world, Chiara's story is a tragedy. After losing two children to rare, life-threatening abnormalities, a young wife and mother dies of cancer to save her son. Where is the hope in that story? Who could find joy in a life like that?

Chiara could, *and she did.* Surrounded by loss and sickness, she found a way to live joyfully by actively receiving whatever God desired to give her with total trust and abandonment. Even when she did not understand, she put her faith in the Lord. She said yes to his will for her.

Here is the interesting thing: when most people hear of Chiara accepting everything from the Lord, they assume that she was accepting from God only trials and heartbreaks. Their minds immediately go to her sufferings. In doing so, they fail to recognize that in addition to trials, God also gave her his grace. He gave her his free and undeserved help to carry her through her trials with peace and even joy. *The reason Chiara was receptive to her crosses was because she was receptive to his grace.*

---

24 Troisi and Paccini, 152.

25 Troisi and Paccini, 152.

God desires to give his grace in everything freely, but he cannot force anyone to receive it. This is the active part of receptivity. He can make his help available, but it has to be accepted. In moments of frustration, anger, and pain, it can be difficult to receive what God is presenting to you with joy. If you have ever felt that way in the past, or maybe you feel that way right now, do not be discouraged.

Even Chiara struggled at times. In losing two children and battling cancer, there were times when she was gloomy, teary, angry, and longing for a normal life. There were times when her cancer treatments left her crying silently, asking God, "Why don't You help me? I know that You can do it!"[26] But what makes Chiara a candidate for sainthood is that she never stayed in that place of frustration or anger. She would always return to a place of receptive trust, knowing that as a child of God, her Father would provide for all her needs.

How Can Receptivity Get Twisted?

Living from a place of active receptivity toward everything the Lord desires to give us is our greatest hope for finding lasting peace and joy. However, sometimes it is difficult to trust that God is working all things for good, so his plans—and subsequent graces—get rejected.

It is so tempting to want to be the authors of our own lives. Especially when what God is leading us to does not make us feel happy in a world that believes personal happiness is the greatest good. But God does not just want to make us happy; he wants to make us holy. He wants to sanctify us.

I know it can be scary to trust in his ways when things do not make sense, but when this happens it is essential to remember

---

26 Troisi and Paccini, 80.

one simple truth: God knows you better than you know yourself. He made you. He formed you in your mother's womb. He knows how many hairs are on your head. If God cares about such a minor detail as that, you can trust that he knows what will make you holy and draw you closer to him. All you have to do is say yes to his will.

Evil and brokenness are never God's plan. In our fallen world, though, bad things can and do happen. In these moments, it can be hard to believe that God will use them for his good. Still, in every circumstance, it is critical to look for how he is working because it is there that peace can be found.

This ability to see God's hand at work was one of Chiara's most extraordinary graces. She was able to see how God used her crosses to sanctify her. Excerpts from a reflection that Chiara wrote on baby Davide explains it all:

> Who is Davide?
>
> A little one who received as a gift from God a very important role: that of knocking down the great Goliaths that are inside each one of us—knocking down our power as parents as we make decisions about him and for him. He showed us that he would grow and that he was like this because God had need of him like this.
>
> He knocked down our "right" to desire a child that was for us, because he was only for God ...
>
> He unmasked the magical faith of the one who thinks he knows God and then asks him to be the candy vending machine.
>
> He demonstrated that God performs miracles, but not with our logical limitations, because God is something greater than our desires (he knocked down the idea of those who seek not salvation of the soul in God, but only that of the body; of all those who ask God for a happy and simple life that does not at all resemble the life of the cross that Jesus left us).

Davide, so little, hurled himself with strength against our idols and cried out with strength in the face of those who did not wish to see; he forced so many to run for shelter in order not to recognize their defeat.

And I thank God for having been defeated by little Davide; I thank God that the Goliath that was inside me is now finally dead, thanks to Davide. No one has succeeded in convincing me that what was happening was a misfortune ... I thank God that my Goliath is finally dead.[27]

What Can We Do About It?

Learning to receive all that God desires to give us with trust can seem intimidating. When looking at Chiara's life, it can be easy to think, "I could never do that. I could never be that joyful in suffering. I could never be that courageous and trusting." But the truth is *you can*. In fact, Chiara herself believed you can.

"Chiara would become very angry when anyone attributed to her the special gift of courage, all her own, that permitted her to confront all these challenges ... She always responded that if she could do it, anyone could ... 'We do not feel courageous,' Chiara related at one point, 'because in reality the only thing that we have done is said yes, one step at a time.'"[28]

Living "one step at a time" was a way of life for Chiara and Enrico. They confronted their challenges by taking "small possible steps" (*piccoli passi possibile*, in Italian). Chiara did not magically wake up one day as a saint. What she did was say yes to the small things.

She said, "Yes, Lord" to the suffering she was experiencing in the moment. "Yes, Lord" to the unknown for the time being. "Yes, Lord" to the experience of loss today. If she tried to say a gigantic

---

27 Troisi and Paccini, 70–71.
28 Troisi and Paccini, 8–9.

yes to the life ahead of her, it would have been overwhelming, but if she said yes to only what was right in front of her, it was manageable.

Still, more importantly than saying yes to her sufferings, she also said yes to the graces she received. "Yes, Lord" to the gift of another day with my unborn child. "Yes, Lord" to the strength for another treatment. "Yes, Lord" to the help you have sent in friends and family. For Chiara, even this ability to receive God's help was in itself a grace, and she often asked for "the grace to live grace," [29] or the grace *to receive grace.*

This is how to do it. This is how to become a saint: receive the grace to say yes to small things, both trials and blessings. Put aside your worry about big things; focus on the little. Focus on taking the small possible steps that will add up to a life of receptivity—a life that is ready and willing to receive whatever God has planned.

Receptivity Challenge

For this chapter's challenge, I invite you to find ten times that you can take a small possible step and say "Yes, Lord" to whatever it is that he is presenting to you over the next twenty-four hours.

The good news you just received? "Yes, Lord." The person who is continually interrupting while you are trying to get something done? "Yes, Lord." The peace God is trying to give you so you can stay calm in a tense situation? "Yes, Lord." The sore muscle that is continuously aching? "Yes, Lord." Whatever he presents to you, receive it. Ten times. Keep track for just one day. Try to be receptive to whatever he has planned. If you hit your ten today, maybe do it again tomorrow.

---

29 Troisi and Paccini, 131.

Discussion Questions

1. Do you feel like you identify with the gift of receptivity? Why or why not? What factors in your life have either stifled or encouraged growth in this gift?

2. Have you ever before heard the concept of men as initiators and women as receivers? If not, what are your thoughts? If you had heard of this idea before reading this chapter, has your understanding of it changed? If so, how?

3. What did you find most inspiring about the life of Servant of God Chiara Corbella Petrillo? What lessons on feminine receptivity can you learn from her?

4. In what ways is it difficult to receive both trials and graces in your life? What specific trial or grace are you currently working on saying yes to?

5. What small possible step do you need to take in your life today?

6. What is one way that you can reveal the gift of receptivity to your family, friends, community, or world?

CHAPTER 4

Maternity and St. Elizabeth Ann Seton

When you see the word "mother," what comes to mind? Your mom or grandma? Perhaps the Blessed Virgin Mary or a saint like Mother Teresa? Or maybe your grade school friend's mom who showed up to every class party and sent the best treats for her kid's birthday? (You know the one—the mom every kid wished was her mom?)

Well, for me, the word brings to mind these images plus, depending on the day, a feeling of delight or anxiety. As the mother of four, the role has simultaneously been the best and most challenging role of my life. I cannot help but recognize that the gift of motherhood is something I should never take for granted. With two, five-year gaps between kids, I know the pain of wondering if my years of mothering are ending early and the joy of an unexpected child.

For each of us, the word mother comes with its own thoughts and emotions, which can be both positive and negative. Perhaps this is because motherhood is at the foundation of all of our lives. Each of us began in the wombs of our mothers. Many of our first memories likely include our moms. Over the years, as our understanding of the word expands, so does its complexity.

All Women Are Mothers

God created woman with a sacred space in her body to give life to others. Knowing how immense this responsibility would be, he equipped her with the abilities needed for mothering. Of course, just because every woman has the physical space to become a mother does not mean that every woman will become one. Regardless, the skills and maternal instincts needed for mothering are bestowed on all women.

This means that women with kids are not the only ones who possess the gift of maternity. Single women, married women without kids, professed religious women—indeed, *all* women— have the gift of maternity. As St. Edith Stein put it, every woman has the skills to "cherish, guard, protect, nourish and advance growth ... [in] all those in contact with her."[30]

Once again, as he does with receptivity, God uses a woman's body to express what he stamped on her soul. A woman can physically mother someone, and she can spiritually mother someone. St. John Paul II called this non-physical mothering "spiritual motherhood." In *Mulieris Dignitatem*, he writes of this concept:

> For virginity does not deprive a woman of her prerogatives. Spiritual motherhood takes on many different forms. In the life of consecrated women, for example ... it can express itself as concern for people, especially the most needy: the sick, the handicapped, the abandoned, orphans, the elderly, children, young people, the imprisoned and, in general, people on the edges of society.[31]

Spiritual motherhood is critical for our world because every human needs the love of a mother. In our broken and hurting world, a woman's maternal love can do so much to care for and

---

30 Stein, *Essays on Woman*, 45.

31 John Paul II, *Mulieris Dignitatem* (August 15, 1988), 21, vatican.va

restore the human heart. As John Paul II writes in his *Letter to Women*, spiritual motherhood "has inestimable value for the development of individuals and the future of society."[32]

Additionally, this gift of mothering the world is in part why "God entrusts the human being to [woman] in a special way." John Paul II goes on to explain, "God entrusts every human being to each and every other human being. But this entrusting concerns women in a special way—precisely by reason of their femininity— and this in a particular way determines their vocation."[33]

In other words, what makes women unique from men is their receptive, maternal nature, which is written on their souls and reflected in their bodies. These unique features determine women's vocation to be active receivers and to help others grow by mothering both physically and spiritually. If there is one saint who seamlessly exemplified both of these facets of motherhood, it would be St. Elizabeth Ann Seton.

Meet St. Elizabeth Ann Seton

Many of the holy women featured in this book are here because they are close to me, like Chiara. Elizabeth is no exception. Not only do her birthday and the anniversary of my engagement fall on the same day, but my ancestors lived and socialized in the same circles as she did in New York, which means they may have known each other. Finally, a piece of Elizabeth is with me, literally. One of our greatest family treasures is a first-class relic of her, and I have rested this encased relic on my laptop as I write.

St. Elizabeth Ann Bayley Seton was born into a well-off New York Protestant family on the brink of the American Revolution in 1774. When she was three years old, her affectionate mother, Catherine

---

32   John Paul II, *Letter to Women*, 9.

33   John Paul II, *Mulieris Dignitatem*, 30.

Charlton Bayley, fell gravely ill and passed away, leaving behind her husband and three daughters. Shortly after her mother's death, her father, Richard Bayley, remarried nineteen-year-old Charlotte Barclay. After a happy start to childhood, Elizabeth's life soon evolved into family dysfunction.

Although Elizabeth and her physician father bonded over a passionate love of learning, he was a workaholic who often left for long stretches to continue his studies in England. He also developed a suspicious friendship with a woman named Mary Fitch. Separated from her estranged husband in Jamaica, Mary lived alone in New York. She was around so much that Elizabeth fondly called her "Mama Fitch." However, years later, after Elizabeth herself had married and made Mary the godmother of her first child, "Mama Fitch" gave birth to a child by Elizabeth's father.

While the true nature of the friendship between Elizabeth's father and Mary Fitch would only be revealed in the future, Elizabeth's stepmother, Catherine, felt her husband's physical and emotional distance. Additionally, as she bore Richard six children, "something in her own temperament—an unhappiness that grew more pronounced as the years passed—left her struggling to nurture her stepdaughters and even her own children."[34] This unhappiness led to her "acting like a drunkard," which was likely the result of an opium addiction.[35]

In her husband's medical supplies, the addictive painkiller laudanum was readily available to Catherine, and she seems to have taken advantage of it. Elizabeth's older sister Mary likely shared this addiction, leaving Elizabeth deeply grieved by her home life. In her pain, she dreamed of escaping to a place "where

---

34 Catherine O'Donnell, *Elizabeth Seton: American Saint* (Ithaca, NY: Cornell University Press, 2018), 26.

35 O'Donnell, 50.

people could be shut up from the world, and pray, and be always good."[36] As a Protestant, such a life seemed impossible to Elizabeth. Though her desires were yet to be purified, the seed of religious life was already growing in her heart.

Sadly, Elizabeth's desire to escape pulled her to the brink of despair. At her lowest point, Elizabeth contemplated suicide through the very source of her sorrows, laudanum. Overdosing on the drug would have been easy to accomplish, yet as she held the bottle, God's grace brought her to put it down.

A New Home

At the age of nineteen, Elizabeth eagerly left her childhood home to marry William Magee Seton. William was a wealthy transatlantic shipping merchant, and she loved him deeply. Together they took up residence on Wall Street where neighbor Alexander Hamilton lived up at one end of the street, and Aaron Burr lived at the other end. Finally, content with life, Elizabeth felt like she had a real home—especially as it began to fill with children.

The contentment did not last for long, however, as tragedy struck the Seton family. William's father, a widower, was involved in a freak accident that resulted in his untimely death. As the oldest of the Seton clan, William took over the family's perilous shipping business, and he became the guardian of his six youngest half-siblings. Suddenly, at the age of twenty-four, Elizabeth became a mother of eight, with another on the way.

These high-stress life changes left Elizabeth describing herself as "woefully fatigued" at times.[37] Even before the addition of William's siblings, Elizabeth had moments of feeling ill-equipped as a mother. Now the weight of this task seemed overwhelming.

---

36 O'Donnell, 52.
37 O'Donnell, 75.

As she wrote to her friend Julia, "To be sure, for me who so dearly loves quiet and a small Family to become at once the Mother of six [additional] children and the Head of so large a number is a very great change. Death or Bread and Water, would be a happy prospect in comparison."[38]

Things went from bad to worse for Elizabeth as William began to exhibit signs of tuberculosis (or consumption) and his shipping business, which was continually hit by pirates and poor investments, was forced to file for bankruptcy. Yet, God's hand was in it all.

With nowhere else to turn, Elizabeth began to open herself up to the Lord. Attending church, reading the Bible, and having conversations about spiritual topics with her sister-in-law Rebecca became routine. For a woman who had been raised nominally Protestant and spent her whole life believing that religion was a nice way for some people to find harmony, these actions were revolutionary. As her faith deepened, her desire to leave this world changed from trying to escape suffering to longing for heaven, which she now saw as her true home.

A Home in Rome

In an effort to improve her husband's health, in 1803, Elizabeth, William, and their oldest daughter traveled to Italy, where the climate was said to be more suited for those with tuberculosis. When they arrived, the government forced them into a twenty-five-day quarantine due to William's sickly disposition. Rather than gleaning any benefit from the Italian air, the Setons remained in a cold, stone room. William's health rapidly declined, and two weeks after the quarantine ended, he passed away.

While the trip did not bring the recovery they had hoped for,

---

38   O'Donnell, 74.

Elizabeth remained in Italy for four more months. During this time, William's former business associates, the Filicchis, introduced Elizabeth to the Catholic Faith. Upon her return to New York, after a series of spiritual twists and turns, Elizabeth shocked her family and friends when, in 1805, she became a Catholic.

Anti-Catholic prejudices were rampant in Protestant New York. As a poor widow, Elizabeth tried to support her children by starting schools, but the projects repeatedly failed due to her new religious beliefs. Even her extended family struggled to understand her decision as they financially sustained her. It soon became apparent that Elizabeth was no longer welcomed in New York society, so she began to look for ways to immerse herself in a Catholic culture and still live her vocation as a mother. Providentially, in 1807, Bishop John Carroll approved a plan for Elizabeth to begin a Catholic girl's school in Maryland that would allow for just that.

After his passing, William's half-siblings that he and Elizabeth had taken in had already settled into new situations. Her two biological sons, now aged ten and twelve, were accepted into a Catholic boys' boarding school a short walk from their future home. Her three daughters (ages thirteen, eight, and six) would be able to attend the Catholic girls' school that Elizabeth was founding. With everything settled, Elizabeth uprooted from New York and headed south.

This definitive move was the starting point of a new life for Elizabeth. Space does not permit a complete account, but the final twelve years of her life have left a legacy that endures throughout the United States. (A brief summary follows, but I encourage you to learn more of the inspiring details.)

After a year of teaching in Baltimore, Elizabeth felt restless as a lay schoolteacher, and she longed to give herself more fully to the Lord. With the Sulpician fathers' help, she envisioned a new sisterhood that would allow her to care for her children and take religious vows. They recruited a handful of founding members, and the United States' first religious order, the Sisters of Charity of St. Joseph, was born. Now an archbishop, John Carroll bestowed on Elizabeth the title of "Mother Seton," and on June 16, 1809, the founding sisters donned the habit Elizabeth had been wearing since her conversion—a simple black dress and bonnet.

The sisters then moved to Emmitsburg, Maryland, where they opened Saint Joseph's Academy and Free School. This school for girls is considered the first Catholic parochial school in the country, making Mother Seton the founder of the Catholic school system in the United States.

As the religious community grew, so did its foundations. In 1814, Mother Seton sent sisters to Philadelphia to establish St. Joseph's Asylum, the first Catholic orphanage in the United States. In 1815, sisters went to Mount St. Mary's to run the infirmary and provide services to the college and seminary. And in 1817, a new orphanage was founded in New York.

In just eleven short years, eighty-six women joined the Sisters of Charity of St. Joseph before Mother Seton, like her husband William, succumbed to tuberculosis at the age of forty-six. Still not done with firsts, St. Elizabeth Ann Seton became the first canonized native-born American saint.

Revealing the Gift of Maternity

To say that Elizabeth's life was impressive would be an understatement. With the feminine genius gift of maternity, she did it all. As the biological mother of five, adoptive mother of six, spiritual mother to hundreds of friends and students, and mother superior of a growing religious community, Elizabeth lived St. Edith Stein's call to "cherish, guard, protect, nourish and advance growth" in every way.

As a mother, Elizabeth loved her children dearly. Their physical and spiritual well-being occupied her heart from the moment of their conceptions. Knowing the pain of growing up with a largely absent father, Elizabeth never considered withdrawing her motherly attention. So, despite her incredible call later in life, she continued to put her children first. As she writes to her friend Julia, "The dear ones have their first claim which must ever remain inviolate. Consequently, if at any period, the duties I am engaged in should interfere with those I owe to them, I have solemnly engaged with our good Bishop John Carroll, as well as my own conscience, to give the darlings their right, and to prefer their advantage in everything."[39]

Elizabeth admitted that she was overwhelmed at first by becoming a mother of eight overnight. This makes her so real. A few months after her new children's arrival, Elizabeth wrote a letter to her half-sister Eliza Sadler that offers a wonderful image of the chaos: "My precious children stick to me like little burrs, they are so fearful of losing me again, the moment I shake one off one side another clings in the opposite, nor can I write one word without some sweet interruption."[40] Regardless of the constant commotion, Elizabeth loved William's brothers and sisters and cared for them with motherly love and attention. As her faith grew, so did her peace and confidence in being a mother of so many.

Later, as a spiritual mother, it seems that Elizabeth benefited from the chaos of her early years of motherhood. When she discovered her call to be a religious sister and educator, she became a mother to many. As she writes, "In the midst of fifty children, I am as a Mother encompassed by many children of different dispositions—

39   Elizabeth Ann Seton, *Elizabeth Bayley Seton: Collected Writings: Volume 2*, ed. Regina Bechtle (Hyde Park, NY: New City Press, 2002), 146.

40   Elizabeth Ann Seton, *Elizabeth Bayley Seton: Collected Writings: Volume 1*, ed. Regina Bechtle (Hyde Park, NY: New City Press, 2000), 21.

not all equally amiable or congenial—but bound to love, instruct, and provide for the happiness of all, to give the example of cheerfulness."[41] Elizabeth took the task of mothering her students seriously, and she remained close to them even after they were no longer her pupils. Additionally, Elizabeth mothered many who joined her in converting to the Catholic Faith, including members of her own extended family.

Finally, as the mother superior of a religious order, Elizabeth truly understood her role to be that of a mother. When she decided to establish a new order, she wrote to her sister-in-law and fellow New York convert, "It is expected I shall be the mother of many daughters."[42] Seeing religious life truly as a sisterhood with a mother at the head, Elizabeth lived this task with great attention and care.

How Can Maternity Get Twisted?

As we all know, society's views on motherhood have changed radically over the past fifty years or so. Until recently, a woman understood that becoming a mother meant co-creating a new life with God. If a woman did not want to get pregnant, then she abstained from having sex. However, if she was married and did seek to get pregnant, then, through sex, she opened herself up to receive new life, knowing ultimately that God, the author of life, would choose whether or not to bless her with the gift of a child. Now, society looks to scientific advances, rather than collaborating with God, as the way to motherhood. Motherhood is seen as an independent right that can be created through artificial means or rejected through contraception or abortion.

Additionally, when it comes to their innate maternal instincts, women are often cued to suppress them in our modern era. For

---

41 Seton, *Collected Writings: Volume 2*, 154.
42 Seton, *Collected Writings: Volume 2*, 34.

example, in the "hook-up" culture, if a woman allows her heart to invest in someone personally, she is bound to get hurt, so she learns to subdue that tendency and keep things superficial. Similarly, if a woman wants to advance in her career, she is encouraged to reject her nurturing instincts and become the "boss witch" who takes charge and gets stuff done.

When you add all of this together, it begs the question, "If God stamped maternity on a woman's soul, then why are women so willing to reject it?" The short answer is that we have free will. Simply because God gives us the gift of maternity (or any other gift of the feminine genius, for that matter), this does not mean we have to receive it.

Men do not always value the complementary, maternal contributions of women and can frequently disregard the need for them. While this is an issue, I think there is something deeper going on that we must first address to untwist a false view of maternity.

In the Church, we hear a lot about "daddy wounds"—that is, how the failings of our fathers or father figures have affected us. For many, these wounds can contribute to a false understanding of who fathers should be and how they should act. However, we do not hear as much about "mommy wounds" and the ways our mothers or mother figures have failed us.

Many of us have been blessed with loving mothers who lived their feminine genius gift of maternity the best they could. Still, no mom is perfect, and even the best have their moments of failure. Broken experiences in our relationships with our mothers can lead to a false view of maternity. In turn, this can lead to a rejection of maternity and fear of motherhood. If this is your experience, please do not give up hope. The story of Elizabeth is proof that there is always hope.

At the tender age of three, Elizabeth lost her mother. Then she had a drug-addicted stepmother who was incapable of nurturing her. Finally, after placing her trust in the unconventional mother figure of "Mama Fitch," she later discovered this "mama" was her father's mistress.

Yet Elizabeth rose above it all. She found a way not to follow the examples of women who failed her. Instead, she became a selfless, nurturing mother to her children, and to countless souls who turned to her for guidance. She found a way to heal and forgive. When her stepmother was on her deathbed, having burned all of her other bridges, it was Elizabeth whom she called on, and Elizabeth "willingly tended her stepmother, giving no thought to the woman's failings during her childhood."[43] Through the grace of God, Elizabeth became Mother Seton.

What Can We Do About It?

Like Elizabeth, reclaiming a true vision of motherhood is possible, but it requires recognizing the ways that our vision is skewed. For those of us with mother wounds, we need to recognize that overcoming them is possible. To do this, each of us must look into our lives and ask the Holy Spirit to reveal to us if anything prevents us from seeing maternity as a gift. We have to ask ourselves how our culture may have falsely shaped our view of maternity and how our mommy wounds may have hindered us from seeing motherhood as it should be.

For some of you, this process may not reveal much, but for others, you may need time to internalize your thoughts or even take them to a spiritual director or Catholic counselor. Whatever the case, do not be afraid to bring your wounds to the light because it is only in the light that they can begin to heal.

It is time to take back and embrace the gift of maternity. Our world needs the love and care of mothers.

---

43   O'Donnell, 184.

Maternity Challenge

The challenge for this chapter is two-fold. First, I invite you to ask the Holy Spirit to reveal to you if you have mommy wounds—from your experiences of our culture or from your experiences with your own mom—that affect your view of maternity. I know this might be an overwhelming task, but this is an essential step if you want to understand your feminine genius. Do not be afraid; God desires your peace, and he will guide you.

Second, just as father wounds can skew our view of God the Father, mother wounds can skew our view of Mary, our heavenly Mother. If you have ever struggled to create a bond with Mary, perhaps it is because you have had a hard time seeing her as a loving mother who cherishes, guards, protects, nourishes, and advances your growth. So, for this challenge, consider setting a "coffee date" with Mary. Bring along your Bible to read some passages that tell her story, and bring your rosary so you can meditate on the life of her Son as she leads you closer to him.

Discussion Questions

1. Can you identify with the gift of maternity? Why or why not? What factors in your life have either stifled or encouraged growth in this gift?

2. Do you have any spiritual mothers in your life? How have they shaped the way you view maternity? What are some ways you have been a spiritual mother to others?

3. What did you find most inspiring about the life of St. Elizabeth Ann Seton? What lessons on the feminine genius gift of maternity can you learn from her?

4. In what ways do you see the gift of maternity being rejected in our world today? What about in your own life?

5. What fears do you have about being a mother? Has our current culture shaped these fears? If yes, in what ways?

6. What is one way that you can reveal the gift of maternity to your family, friends, community, or world?

CHAPTER 5

Sensitivity and Servant of God Dorothy Day

At the beginning of his *Letter to Women*, St. John Paul II writes, "Thank you, women who are daughters and women who are sisters! Into the heart of the family, and then of all society, you bring the richness of your sensitivity, your intuitiveness, your generosity and fidelity."[44] These four gifts of sensitivity, intuition, generosity, and fidelity flow from the gifts of self-giving, receptivity, and maternity. Beginning with sensitivity, we now turn our attention to these gifts.

Gratitude

I have attended, led, or spoken at dozens of women's events over the years. They are among my favorite places to be. I love the ways the hosts of these events attentively care for each woman in attendance. From custom-themed journals and pens to baskets in the restrooms with hand lotion and pain relievers, every detail is thought through. It brings me so much joy to watch as the room fills with warm greetings and laughter. I delight in the tailor made women's talks and relish in the sound of an all-female chorus singing praises to our Lord or reciting the Hail Mary. I love everything about these sacred times, and I am beyond grateful that they are a part of my vocation.

---

44 John Paul II, *Letter to Women*, 2.

During each experience, there is one moment in particular that I love to watch for. If you have attended a similar event, perhaps this is a familiar scene: At the end of the program, a woman gets up to thank everyone who has made the event possible. While sharing gratitude from her heart, tears begin to well up in her eyes. Trying not to cry, she waves her hand at her face, saying, "Um ... I promised myself I wasn't going to do this ... sorry ... it's just that you all are so wonderful, and I'm so grateful and ..." And there it is, the moment I watch for—the crying-while-thanking-people speech. I love it because it is a moment that reveals the gift of feminine genius sensitivity, but maybe not for the reasons you might be thinking.

True Sensitivity

Stereotypical feminine sensitivity is often equated with crying. As I have mentioned, I do not do much of that. In fact, when I recently hosted a women's conference, I did not cry during the thank you speech. Years ago, I would have thought my lack of tears made me less of a woman. However, after reading St. John Paul II's thoughts on sensitivity, I now believe that tears are a *result* of sensitivity rather than a sign of it.

There is nothing wrong with genuine tears. We apologize for them all of the time when, in reality, they are a beautiful expression of love. However, according to John Paul II, the deeper display of sensitivity in a crying-while-thanking-people speech is not the crying; it is the thanking. For John Paul II, feminine genius sensitivity lies in a woman's ability to see and understand each person's needs. Women recognize practical surface needs, such as hand lotion in the bathroom, and deeper interior needs, such as the need to be acknowledged and appreciated for the time, love, and energy spent in putting on a conference.

What makes this sensitivity possible is a woman's unique ability to *"acknowledge the person,* because they see persons with their hearts."[45] This unique feminine gift prompted John Paul II to proclaim that "in a special way the human being is entrusted to woman, precisely because the woman in virtue of her special experience of motherhood is seen to have a *specific sensitivity* toward the human person and all that constitutes the individual's true welfare."[46]

Here, John Paul II says that women are entrusted with humanity because they have the sensitivity needed to care for it. This sensitivity, which flows from their gift of maternity, allows them not only to see others' needs but also to recognize the inherent value and dignity of each person. This means that women tend to view people as *people*, not as objects for personal gain, progress, or selfishness—and not as "less than" because they are not useful in the eyes of the world.

Sadly, the failure to see people as people is a part of everyday life in our modern times. It is visible in working environments, as peers use each other for personal advancement and employers view employees as commodities. It manifests itself in dating when couples use each other for physical and emotional pleasure. It shows itself in the ways people neglect to care for the poor, both physically and spiritually. Finally, it reveals itself when women abort their children conceived in unideal circumstances or with disabilities. In so many ways, humanity has lost its sensitivity to others' worth, value, and dignity.

These trends were of deep concern for St. John Paul II as he watched them "lead to a gradual *loss of sensitivity for man, that is, for what is essentially human.*" In a call for women to rise, he proclaims, "Our time in particular *awaits the manifestation* of that 'genius' which belongs to women, and which can ensure sensitivity for human beings in every circumstance: because they are human!"[47]

---

45   John Paul II, 12.

46   John Paul II, *Christifideles Laici* (December 30, 1988), 51, vatican.va.

47   John Paul II, *Mulieris Dignitatem*, 30.

Now more than ever, our feminine sensitivity is needed, and one woman to turn to for an example of how to reveal this gift is Servant of God Dorothy Day.

Meet Servant of God Dorothy Day

Dorothy Day, a convert to the Faith after a deeply prodigal past, is perhaps the most unique and misunderstood woman up for canonization in the Church today. Depending on the issue, she was too conservative for some, and for others, she was too progressive. Nevertheless, as Cardinal Timothy Dolan puts it, "I am convinced Dorothy is a saint for our time. She exemplifies what's best in Catholic life, the ability we have to be 'both-and' not 'either-or.'"[48] As complex as she is, one thing no one can deny is her love for the poor and her devotion to her Catholic Faith after her conversion.

Experiencing Poverty

Born in 1897, Dorothy was the middle child of five. When she was eight, her family's world was literally rocked by the San Francisco earthquake of 1906. Living across the bay in Oakland, California, Dorothy's family was active in helping the victims as jobless, homeless refugees began traveling across the water. This first experience with the destitute profoundly impacted young Dorothy, who experienced a unique joy while helping aid refugees.

Due to the disaster, the newspaper that employed Dorothy's father, John, was forced to close. Now jobless himself, John moved his family to Chicago in search of work. There, the Days rented a low-income tenement flat, and Dorothy experienced poverty herself. In their pieced together flat, with clothing scraps for curtains and fruit cases for bookshelves, her family's state embarrassed her. When walking home

---

48 Brandon Vogt, *Saints and Social Justice: A Guide to Changing the World* (Huntington, IN: Our Sunday Visitor, 2014), 106–107.

from school with friends, she would enter a nicer apartment building to give the impression that her family was not as poor as it was.

Since Dorothy's parents were not religious, faith was not a part of her home life. However, the Lord revealed himself to her in little ways through friends. She heard about the saints from one, encountered another's mother praying on her knees, and attended an Episcopalian church with a third. Each of these events stirred her heart in ways she did not yet understand.

Searching for More

As a student at the University of Illinois, Dorothy followed in her father's footsteps and pursued a degree in journalism. There she quickly became friends with members of the Socialist Party and eventually became a member herself. During this time, she also wholeheartedly embraced Karl Marx's belief that faith merely gave people the illusion that life was OK despite suffering and injustice. (Marx famously dismisses religion as "the opiate of the people.")

Studying left Dorothy restless and homesick, so halfway through her degree, she dropped out and moved to New York, where her family had relocated. She began taking freelance jobs writing for socialist and left-wing newspapers, covering demonstrations and interviewing leaders of reform movements. Moved by their passion, Dorothy became more involved in social activism. At the same time, though, she found herself drawn toward the beauty of Catholic liturgy. After spending all night drinking in bars, it was not unusual for her to kneel in the shadows at any early morning Mass before heading home.

As Dorothy's career began to grow, her life began to be filled with drama and heartbreak. While covering a suffragette demonstration, she was arrested with thirty-five other women and sentenced to thirty days in jail. The women collectively protested their treatment and went on a hunger strike. This action landed them in solitary confinement, and the only book the guards would give Dorothy was a Bible. She tried to convince herself she was reading for "literary enjoyment," but in her state of desolation, the words resonated with her heart.[49]

Months later, the Spanish Flu pandemic of 1918 hit, and hospitals were desperate for nurses due to World War I and an overall shortage of staff. Answering the call, Dorothy took a break from writing and became a nurse. While at the hospital, she tended to a man named Lionel Moise and soon fell madly in love. Although she desperately wanted to marry him, he kept reminding her that their relationship was just a casual affair. So, when Dorothy found herself pregnant, she knew Lionel would abandon her if she kept the child.

Dorothy was torn. Even without any religious convictions regarding the sanctity of life, she was deeply troubled by the idea of aborting her unborn child.[50] Despite her hesitations, her fear of losing Lionel was greater. She allowed him to take her to get an abortion, and he promised he would be back to pick her up. When he never showed, Dorothy took a cab home and found a note from him explaining that he had left New York and had no intention of returning.

Heartbroken and vulnerable, Dorothy quickly met and married Berkeley Tobey, who was sixteen years older than her and had been divorced three times. Before their nearly year-long honeymoon in Europe was even complete, Berkeley's fourth marriage had ended as well.

Next, Dorothy headed to Chicago, where she found lodging at a boardinghouse run by a socialist group that was closely watched by the authorities. During her first night's stay, the police raided the house and arrested Dorothy on false charges of prostitution.

---

49 Dorothy Day, *The Long Loneliness* (New York: Harper and Brothers, 1952), 81.

50 At that time, abortion was illegal (without exceptions) in all fifty states.

Although the prostitution charges were quickly dropped, the culmination of these rapid-fire events left Dorothy battered in spirit. It was not until a movie studio bought the rights to one of her novels that she finally found a semblance of outward calm. The influx of cash allowed her to return to New York and buy a cabin by the ocean. In the quiet, the Lord was finally able to water the seeds he had been planting in Dorothy's heart. Daily walks on the beach afforded her time to pray, and she started attending Mass on Sundays.

Soon Dorothy found a new man to love named Forster Batterham. But Forster was an atheist and an anarchist, so he often challenged Dorothy on her pull toward the Catholic Faith. A few years into their relationship, Dorothy became pregnant. While Forster was not interested in becoming a father, Dorothy was elated and refused to consider having another abortion. Her daughter Tamar was born on March 4, 1926, and Dorothy gave her the middle name of Teresa after St. Teresa of Avila.

Motherhood changed something in Dorothy. Her faith began to deepen, and she wanted to have Tamar Teresa baptized in the Catholic Church. She knew that this would jeopardize her relationship with Forster, but she went ahead nonetheless—and, a year later, Dorothy herself entered the Church. As she expected, her relationship with Forster came to an end.

The Catholic Worker

Now tasked with providing for Tamar as a single mother, Dorothy began moving about to chase after work. The Great Depression was underway, and despite her own struggles to get by, the plight of the poor weighed heavily on her heart. As Dorothy considered her radical friends—who were socialists, anarchists, and atheists—she felt uneasy that they, as non-believers, were fighting to bring dignity, work, and food to the poor while she, a believing Catholic, stood by watching. As she writes, "How little, how puny my work had been since becoming a Catholic. How self-centered, how ingrown, how lacking in sense of community! ... My self-absorption seemed sinful as I watched my brothers in their struggle, not for themselves, but for others."[51]

One night, after covering a Hunger March in Washington, DC, she went to the National Shrine of the Immaculate Conception to attend Mass. Restless about her situation, Dorothy recalls, "There I offered up a special prayer, a prayer which came with tears and with anguish, that some way would open up for me to use what talents I possessed for my fellow workers, for the poor."[52]

In answer to her prayer, the very next day a man named Peter Maurin showed up at her door. Peter was familiar with Dorothy's work as a journalist and asked her to join him in founding a social justice movement rooted in the Gospel and Catholic social teachings. The two got to work right away and established *The Catholic Worker* newspaper, which was aimed at educating readers on the conditions of the working poor and inspire them to put Catholic social teachings into action.

As support for the publication grew, others began to join them, and the *Catholic Worker* movement was born. With Peter and Dorothy at the helm, the community worked tirelessly to advocate for the needy, especially the working poor. From organizing boycotts and strikes for the overworked and underpaid to creating houses of hospitality and farming communities for the hungry and needy, *Catholic Worker* community members aimed to live daily the corporal works of mercy.

For nearly fifty years, Dorothy organized, protested, marched, served, spoke, and wrote to combat injustice for the sake of the Gospel. At seventy-six, she went to jail for the last of eleven times, and she finally

---

51   Dorothy Day, 165.
52   Dorothy Day, 165.

stepped down as a leader for the movement a year later. She passed away peacefully on November 29, 1980, at the age of eighty-three.

To this day, *The Catholic Worker* newspaper continues in its mission. Dorothy's devotion to Jesus and his Church, as well as how she used her feminine sensitivity to understand and passionately fight for the needs of those she served, lives on through various *Catholic Worker* communities.[53]

Revealing the Gift of Sensitivity

From a young age, Dorothy's feminine genius gift of sensitivity manifested itself in her concern for others' well-being. Even without a religious doctrine to guide her, she innately believed that every human had the right to be treated with dignity and equality. In these early years, her conclusions about how best to achieve these aims were sometimes misguided—even deeply flawed—but she was sensitive to the human needs of the poor and fought to bring them food, shelter, and work.

Without the strength of God's sacramental grace, Dorothy silenced her innate sensitivity when she chose to abort her first child. Her sensitivity to her unborn child's needs was present—she knew something was not right about killing her baby—but she could not find the strength or support to choose life. Allowing fear to suppress the voice within her that said "this is a child," her choice had tragic consequences for the unborn child and herself. Dorothy would keenly feel the pain of this decision, later referring to it as the greatest tragedy of her life.[54]

When given a second chance, under similar circumstances, Dorothy chose life for her daughter Tamar and never allowed

---

53 *Note:* These communities are autonomous, so they vary in their interpretation of the organization's tenants and in their fidelity to the teachings of the Church.

54 Terrence C. Wright, *Dorothy Day: An Introduction to Her Life and Thought* (San Francisco: Ignatius Press, 2018), 28.

her views on abortion to be left to question. For example, after the release of *Humanae Vitae*, which unequivocally declared the Church's pro-life and anti-contraception stance, she wrote, "Thank God we have a Pope Paul who upholds *respect for life*, an ideal so lofty, so high, so important even when it seems he has the whole Catholic world against him."[55]

The brokenness of Dorothy's prodigal years runs deep, and we should never make light of the suffering she must have experienced as a result. She was a real woman, not a fictional character in a conversion novel. Her story illustrates that truth that even when we make choices that distance ourselves from God, he finds a way to use our broken decisions for his greater glory.

Post-Conversion Sensitivity

While Dorothy always had a sensitivity to others' physical and social needs, it was not until after her conversion that her sensitivity to their deeper, spiritual needs blossomed. In 1940, Dorothy published the "Aims and Purposes" of the *Catholic Worker*. Her strong words can leave no doubt that the spiritual works of mercy were just as much a part of her efforts as the corporal works of mercy:

> Together with the Works of Mercy, feeding, clothing and sheltering our brothers, we must indoctrinate. We must "give reason for the faith that is in us." Otherwise we are scattered members of the Body of Christ, we are not "all members one of another." Otherwise, our religion is an opiate, for ourselves alone, for our comfort ...
>
> If we do not keep indoctrinating, we lose the vision. And if we lose the vision, we become merely philanthropists, doling out palliatives ...
>
> This work of ours toward a new heaven and a new earth shows a correlation between the material and the spiritual, and, of course, recognizes the primacy of the spiritual. Food for the body is not

---

55 Dorothy Day, "A Reminiscence at 75," *Commonweal Magazine*, August 10, 1973, commonwealmagazine.org/.

enough. There must be food for the soul. Hence the leaders of the work, and as many as we can induce to join us, must go daily to Mass, to receive food for the soul ... If we lose faith, if we stop the work of indoctrinating, we are in a way denying Christ again.[56]

Dorothy's sensitivity understood the "primacy of the spiritual." She recognized that the most profound need of those she served was an encounter with Christ.

How Can Sensitivity Get Twisted?

As with all feminine genius gifts, revealing sensitivity to the world is a unique privilege. A woman's awareness of the needs of others is imperative for achieving a just society. However, danger can arise when her propensity to be sensitive to others' needs leads to a disproportionate sensitivity to her own needs.

As the chapter on self-giving highlighted, each of us has legitimate needs that must be addressed. Taking care of ourselves is essential, but it is equally essential to ensure that our concern for ourselves does not become obsessive and self-absorbed. As St. John Paul II warns, "The woman, as much as the man, must take care that her sensitivity does not succumb to the temptation to possessive selfishness, and must put it at the service of authentic love. On these conditions she gives of her best."[57]

It can be all too easy to allow sensitivity to become self-centered. When this happens, our focus shifts from the thoughts and feelings of others to our own. We can be tempted to focus solely on how things may or may not affect us or what are simply our wants or needs. While this egocentric tendency is all too human, it causes a two-fold problem.

---

56 Dorothy Day, "Aims and Purposes," *The Catholic Worker*, February 7, 1940, catholicworker.org/.

57 John Paul II, General Audience (July 23, 1995), in *John Paul II Speaks on Women*, para. 2.

First, when we are fixated on ourselves, it becomes difficult to think about others. This makes it easy to forget that our lives are to be a gift of self to the people God has entrusted to us.

Second, being self-focused makes it easy to zoom in on the flaws in our lives and harbor a victim attitude that is neither helpful nor productive. "My life is so challenging. Everything is unfair to me. Why am I the only one dealing with this?" This type of negative self-talk can breed bitterness and ingratitude, and it prevents us from being receptive to the graces God desires to give us to aid us in our trials.

Some have heavier crosses than others, and I know many of you are hurting in profound ways. The brokenness of this world is real, and the weight it can bear upon our lives can be substantial. However, you do not need to spend the rest of your life living from your wounds. With the Lord's help, you can gain the freedom to look beyond your crosses. With his help, you can gain the freedom to stop looking down and in and start looking up and out.

That is the freedom that Dorothy Day breathed. Living through the Great Depression as a single mother because the baby's father left her when she chose to follow Jesus and become Catholic gave her every reason to turn in on herself. Yet, she chose not to. Instead, she used her broken experiences to heighten her sensitivity toward the needs of others.

Think about it. It was because of her experiences serving the homeless after the San Francisco earthquake, living in poverty in a Chicago tenement, serving jail time with broken women, living paycheck to paycheck to provide for her daughter ... all of these circumstances are what heightened her sensitivity to the needs of others and compelled her to respond with love. While her abortion and divorce were never God's will for her life, he found a way to use them to heighten her sensitivity in the most painful of circumstances. Instead of turning in on the hurt and pain, Dorothy learned to look up and out and to ask, "What can I do? How can I make things better?"

Suffering, trials, heartbreaks, and setbacks are never God's perfect will for us. They are his *permissive* will, and if it is possible to allow him to make something beautiful out of the broken, our sensitivity to others' needs can make the world better.

What Can We Do About It?

As St. John Paul II says, each of us is called to place our sensitivity "at the service of authentic love." However, because our tendency is to place our sensitivity at the service of ourselves, this is easier said than done. How can we stop focusing on ourselves and start focusing on others? For this task, here are three simple ideas.

First, recognize that selfless sensitivity only happens with God's grace. The Lord is not asking you to muster up a brute force of the will to think of others before you think of yourself. His grace is always available if you are open to receiving it. Call on him when you are finding it difficult to move beyond yourself.

Second, use your personal experiences to understand the needs of others. If you have ever felt lonely, seek those who have been left out and include them. If you have ever experienced loss, look for those who are grieving and comfort them. If you have ever struggled with doubt, find the despairing and bring them hope. Each of us has personal experiences that can relate to those in need.

Third, start small. Call a friend who is struggling to let them know they are not alone. Keep essential items such as soft foods and bottled water in your car to pass out to the homeless, so they know they are not invisible. Look someone in the eyes when they talk to you, so they know you are genuinely listening. Apologize and make amends when you have hurt someone to let them know they deserve to be treated with dignity. These small acts might not seem like much, but when you add them together, they build a life of sensitivity toward the deeper needs of others.

Sensitivity Challenge

In Dorothy's unrest over her inaction as a Catholic who felt called to love the poor, she prayed, "Lord, open up a way for me to use what talents I possess for the poor."

Today I invite you to ask yourself, "Who is the Lord calling me to love?" Right now, brainstorm a list of individuals, groups, organizations, or movements that could use your intentional feminine sensitivity.

Does God need your sensitivity to love the underserved youth of your parish? A coworker who is struggling? The pro-life movement? Your local St. Vincent de Paul Society? Young adults who long for community? Your husband, who might not always find the words to ask for your support? Or your children, who may always seem to be needy? Whatever comes to mind, write all of your ideas down and ask the Lord where he is calling you to reveal your feminine sensitivity. Then take a deep breath and sincerely pray Dorothy's prayer, "Lord, open up a way for me to use what talents I possess for _____."

Discussion Questions

1. Can you identify with the gift of sensitivity? Why or why not? What factors in your life have either stifled or encouraged growth in this gift?

2. According to St. John Paul II, sensitivity is the ability to understand the human heart's deeper needs. How does this definition differ from the world's definition of sensitivity? Do you feel like you possess sensitivity in the way John Paul II defined it? Why or why not?

3. What did you find most inspiring about the life of Servant of God Dorothy Day? What lessons on the feminine genius gift of sensitivity can you learn from her?

4. Are there times when your sensitivity picks up on someone else's needs but you fail to acknowledge or respond to it? What holds you back?

5. Did you pray the prayer suggested in the chapter's challenge? If so, how might the Lord be calling you to reveal the gift of sensitivity at this time in your life to your family, friends, community, or world?

CHAPTER 6

Intuition and St. Catherine of Siena

As part of my research for this book, I hosted a weekly feminine genius small group. Each Sunday, ten young adult women sat in my living room drinking sparkling water and eating baked goods as we discussed one feminine genius gift per meeting. Not only was it a great way to ensure my house got a decent weekly cleaning, but it also provided an invaluable treasure trove of personal insights and lived feminine genius experiences.

When the week came to talk about intuition, everyone in the group agreed that they felt like they possessed it, but no one was sure how to define it. Some commented that it is kind of like your instincts, conscience, or the promptings of the Holy Spirit trying to guide you in the right direction. Others likened it to sensitivity, in the sense that intuition helps people identify the needs of others. Yet, someone noted, in his *Letter to Women*, St. John Paul II lists this gift separately when he thanked women for their sensitivity, intuitiveness, generosity, and fidelity. While intuition seemed hard to pin down, in the end, everyone agreed that intuition is that thing you get when you *just know*.

Intuition and Science

I think the ladies in my small group were right on. In fact, according to Dr. Greg Bottaro of the CatholicPsych Institute, scientific research on the female brain backs up the theory that sometimes women *just know.*

The brain consists of both gray matter and white matter. Gray matter is composed mostly of neuron cell bodies, and white matter is composed mostly of these cell bodies' long arms, which facilitate cell communication. These arms work like communication tracks that connect cells together. When it comes to areas of the brain that have to do with higher-order thinking, women have ten times more white matter than men. This means that when women are thinking, they are quickly gathering and inputting data from a variety of cells and sources. Additionally, as they make these connections, women especially draw from their brain's right side. As Dr. Bottaro explained, processing information this way "allows women to pick up on more cues about the outside world and connect them" and thus, "women draw conclusions from many areas of experience, sometimes without even knowing how or why, which is why their intuition is better developed." [58]

It is unclear whether St. John Paul II knew about the science behind women's intuition, but he certainly was not grasping at straws by highlighting it. As Dr. Bottaro told me, sometimes women just "*know*" without knowing how they know.[59] No wonder the women in my group could not pin down an exact definition!

Intuition and John Paul II

In addition to wiring intuition into a woman's brain, the Lord also wired it into her heart. In *Mulieris Dignitatem,* John Paul II

---

58 Gregory Bottaro, "Cold, Hard Proof of John Paul II's 'Feminine Genius,'" *Aleteia,* August 31, 2015, aleteia.org/.

59 Gregory Bottaro, email message to author, March 12, 2021.

writes regarding a mother's intuitive ability to recognize the gift of new life growing inside her: "Motherhood involves a special communion with the mystery of life, as it develops in the woman's womb. The mother is filled with wonder at this mystery of life, and 'understands' with unique intuition what is happening inside her." [60] Here John Paul II puts quotations around the word "understands" to acknowledge that none of us can fully grasp the miracle of life; before even meeting her child, however, a mother intuitively knows that it is her responsibility to protect and nourish the invisible life growing inside of her.

Here, spiritual motherhood once again comes into play, as this intuition to nourish and protect life is not reserved for physical mothers only. Returning to *On the Collaboration of Men and Women in the Church and in the World*, Pope Benedict XVI highlights how feminine intuition is present in all life-giving activities:

> Among the fundamental values linked to women's actual lives is what has been called a "capacity for the other." Although a certain type of feminist rhetoric makes demands "for ourselves," women preserve the deep intuition of the goodness in their lives of those actions which elicit life, and contribute to the growth and protection of the other.

> This intuition is linked to women's physical capacity to give life. Whether lived out or remaining potential, this capacity is a reality that structures the female personality in a profound way. It allows her to acquire maturity very quickly, and gives a sense of the seriousness of life and of its responsibilities. [61]

In other words, Benedict says that a woman's intuitive desire to care for others goes against modern notions that push for women to care only for themselves. A woman's intuition tells her that she was made to give of herself to others. This intuition tells her she was made for life-giving actions that help others to grow and

---

60 John Paul II, *Mulieris Dignitatem*, 18.

61 Ratzinger and Amato, 13.

develop into who they were made to be and this is a direct result of her capacity to give life physically. Knowledge of this call to selflessly bring life into the world explains why women mature quickly and take their responsibilities seriously.

In sum, because women intuitively know they need to care for others, and because their brains instinctively connect dots quickly, when it comes to people, sometimes women "just know" what needs to be done and how to do it.

All Spheres of Society

Understanding the importance of feminine intuition, which stems from the gift of maternity and is heightened by feminine sensitivity, is one of many reasons why St. John Paul II stresses the need for women to be present in all spheres of society.

Many times he invites women to "increasingly play a part in the solutions of the serious problems of the future."[62] Or he would begin a speech by saying, "I would like to stress the importance of a greater involvement of women in public life."[63] In a variety of ways he asked people, "How can we fail to see that, in order to deal satisfactorily with the many problems emerging today, special recourse to the feminine genius is essential?"[64]

John Paul II believed that the influence and voice of women were essential in all spheres of society. In bringing their genius to public life, women humanize plans, policies, and decisions. They ensure that each person is valued and given dignity.

This means that bringing your feminine genius into society

---

62 John Paul II, *Letter to Women*, 4.

63 John Paul II, "Angelus" (August 27, 1995), in *John Paul II Speaks on Women*, para. 1.

64 John Paul II, "Angelus" (August 20, 1995), in *John Paul II Speaks on Women*, para. 1.

extends beyond baking cookies for company birthday celebrations or bringing in flowers to brighten up a workspace. While these types of beautiful feminine touches are small acts of love that truly humanize work environments, they are not the only way women can use their intuition in the public sphere.

In addition to attending to the little things, bringing feminine intuition into all spheres of society means not being afraid to push back when a new policy is insensitive to the human needs of your clients and employees. It means offering a respectful but different perspective if barriers will prevent those who need your services from obtaining them. It means advocating for your children's health or education if they are not receiving the attention they need. It means speaking up and expressing concerns for those not in the room to speak for them. It means voicing your intuition when you know a decision is about to be made that is not best for all parties involved. A female saint who lived this kind of feminine intuition well was St. Catherine of Siena.

Meet St. Catherine of Siena

Though she was physically short in stature, St. Catherine of Siena was a spiritual giant among the giants. She was canonized by Pope Pius II in 1461, only eighty-one years after her death. In 1866, she was declared a patron saint of Rome, and in 1939, co-patron saint of Italy (along with St. Francis of Assisi). In 1999, she was declared a co-patron saint of Europe. In addition, just one week after naming St. Teresa of Avila the first female Doctor of the Church in 1970, the Church bestowed the same honor on St. Catherine of Siena.

In 2012, my husband and I had the blessed opportunity to visit Catherine's hometown of Siena. Stepping into the heart of her city is a bit of a time warp. Due to the bubonic plague, which reached Siena in 1348, the town lost two-thirds of its population and never fully returned to its former days of glory. However, for a tourist and devotee of Catherine, this makes for an idyllic pilgrimage. Portions of her family's large home still stand, with much of it converted into chapels. The Basilica of St. Dominic, where she frequently attended Mass and prayed, still towers over the city from its hilltop perch. There you can venerate Catherine's incorrupt head, and her right thumb—the rest of her body is mostly in Rome with the exception of a few small appendages in Venice. If you are ever in Italy, a visit to Siena is well worth the stop, and knowing Catherine's story makes it all the more special.

The Life of a Tiny Giant

St. Catherine of Siena was the twenty-fourth of twenty-five children born to Giacomo Benincasa and Lapa di Puccio dé Piacenti in 1347. As a child, Catherine was known for her great joy and piety. When she was six, Jesus appeared to her for the first of many times, and when she was seven, she took a vow of virginity, promising to give her whole life to God. As she came of age, however, her parents were eager to find her a husband. This greatly grieved Catherine, so to make herself look less desirable, she chopped her hair down to the scalp and began to wear a head covering. After much struggle over the matter, her parents eventually relented and allowed her to keep her promise to God.

Assured that she would not be forced to marry, Catherine began to beg her parents to help her join the Sisters of Penance of St. Dominic. These women, called the Mantellata, followed the rule of St. Dominic and wore habits, but, unlike today's sisters, they lived at home and were comprised of "respectable widows of mature age who wanted to dedicate themselves to the service of God."[65] To admit a young virgin like Catherine into their order was unprecedented. Still, the Mantellata agreed that if she was

---

65   Raymond of Capua, *The Life of St. Catherine of Siena*, trans. George Lamb (Charlotte, NC: TAN Books, 1934), 44–45.

not too pretty, they could accept her because then her acceptance would likely not lead to a future scandal.

Upon taking the habit, Catherine began living in silence and solitude. During this time of intense prayer and penance, she experienced "heavenly visions, revelations and visits from the Lord."[66] From them, she gained deep spiritual insights and an inseparable unity with Jesus. After three years in solitude, only leaving her room to receive the sacraments, she heard the Lord call her out of her seclusion and back into public life. Since she was hesitant to go, Jesus assured her that he would never part from her. Catherine now had a mission to bring Jesus, whom she knew so intimately, into the world.

Reentering society, Catherine served her large family by doing menial chores, and she attended to her wider community by caring for the sick and needy. Her heroic virtue was great in these areas, but soon the Lord called her to widen her scope by acting as a peacemaker in family and political feuds. Her skills in this delicate task were so strong that when the Florentines were at odds with the papacy, they sent Catherine to represent them before Pope Gregory XI.

To visit the pope, Catherine did not go to Rome, however. She had to go to Avignon, which was part of the Holy Roman Empire and under the influence of France. Decades before, politically charged circumstances led to the controversial relocation of the papacy to Avignon, a move that was a source of frustration for many in Christendom. Taking advantage of the trip that brought her to Avignon, Catherine urged the pontiff to return to Rome to heal the division to the Church. At first, he resisted her pleas, but after three months of persistent encouragement, the papal court moved back to Rome after a seventy-one-year absence.

---

66   Raymond of Capua, 56.

Shortly after the pope's return to Rome, a new concern for the Church arose. Pope Gregory XI passed away, and his successor, Pope Urban VI, quickly made enemies with several cardinals. The cardinals did not approve of Urban VI's reform efforts, so they elected their own "pope," Clement VII. This move divided the Church and put countries, cities, religious orders, and families at odds. Bereaved by this division, Catherine moved to Rome at the request of the rightful Pope Urban VI. There she tirelessly worked to restore unity in the Church by writing letters, meeting with cardinals, and prayerfully supporting Urban VI.

In 1380, at the age of thirty-three, Catherine sensed that her time on earth was limited. She gathered those close to her and from her deathbed "she delivered a long memorable speech to [those present], encouraging them to persevere in virtue."[67] Hours later, she departed this world to achieve her final unity with her Spouse in heaven.

Catherine's life as a mystic, miracle worker, and prophetess can make her biography, written by her confessor, Blessed Raymond of Capua, seem more like pious Catholic fiction than fact. Yet Catherine was very real, and so was the way God worked through her. Her incredible wisdom and holiness left clergy in awe. The ways she lovingly performed acts of charity and penance dumbfound people to this day.

There is so much more that we could explore her gifts for pages. However, for our purposes, let us move forward to uncover her feminine genius intuition, particularly looking at how Catherine brought this gift into the public sphere.

Revealing the Gift of Intuition

As a mystic, Catherine frequently dialogued directly with Jesus, so at times her gifts did admittedly go beyond ordinary feminine

---

67   Raymond of Capua, 301.

gifts. When it comes to Catherine's intuition, it is impossible to separate out when Jesus was supernaturally directing her and when Catherine was simply following her intuition. Yet Catherine's own thoughts, cultural influences, and personality surface in her hundreds of letters. As one historian notes,

> Her concerns were mystical and pastoral. And the pastoral finds its finest expression in these letters of hers, where she shares the amazing synthesis of her own thought ... Hers is a common-sense yet uncompromising spirituality.[68]

This indicates that while Catherine did at times get a hearty dose of supernatural direction from Jesus, her unique feminine intuition was utilized as she worked to serve, teach, and advise those who came to her.

Together with the mystical gifts Our Lord gave her, Catherine's ability to intuitively know what to do in many circumstances, especially concerning human relationships, helped bring peace to both the public and private spaces where she ministered to others. As Pope Pius II attested in the document of Catherine's canonization,

> She assisted the unfortunate and the oppressed, converted sinners, and attracted them to penance by the mildness of her discourse; she gave counsel with joy, and indicated to each one what he should do and what he should avoid—she calmed disputants, appeased a great number of violent hatreds and terminated many bloody enmities ... two Roman Pontiffs, Gregory XI and Urban VI, esteemed her so highly that they charged her with several negotiations.[69]

Catherine's intuition shined in the way she cared for others' physical and spiritual needs, especially the poor. It shined in the

---

68 Catherine of Siena, *The Letters of St. Catherine of Siena: Volume 1*, trans. Suzanne Noffke, OP (Binghamton, NY: MRTS, 1988), 8.

69 http://www.drawnbylove.com/BullofPiusII_06191461.pdf.

way she counseled men and women from all walks of life as she
inspired them to commit themselves more fully to the Lord. And it
shined in the way she negotiated peace between warring families
and communities.

Catherine's sweeping contributions to the Church and the society
of her day showcase the way feminine genius intuition can bear
fruit, especially in the public sphere where she "play[ed] a part
in the solutions of the serious problems" that faced her society.[70]

How Can Intuition Get Twisted?

Feminine intuition has the power to understand needs and
situations without calculated analysis. This unique propensity
is a gift, but a woman must be aware that her intuition has the
potential to make her prideful in thinking she always knows the
correct answer. This twisting of a gift can lead her to believe that
others, especially men, are kind of stupid because what may seem
evident to her is not obvious to others.

Let me give you an example. When first-time parents bring home
a newborn baby, they are both overwhelmed, but the mom kind
of knows what to do—a special motherly intuition kicks in. So
when dad is taking care of the baby, she cannot help telling him
what to do. This intuition can result in her correcting him every
time he tries to do something. "When you change her diaper,
don't forget to do this," or "When you're putting her to sleep,
make sure you do that." While mom is only trying to pass on her
intuitive knowledge, sometimes this imparting of wisdom feels
more like nagging or belittling, and over time dad begins to lose
his confidence in parenting.

The same sort of thing can happen in dating relationships.
Sometimes women intuitively know what needs to happen in

70   John Paul II, *Letter to Women*, 4.

a relationship. Perhaps a relationship needs to move to the next level, or a couple needs to incorporate their faith more or find ways to communicate better. These changes might seem obvious to a woman, but her sweetheart might not always see it. When this happens, women are often tempted to try to drag guys into doing the right thing. While these women might be right about what needs to be done, it is important to allow men to step up on their own. If a woman tries to drag her guy along, he might fail to develop in ways that help him come to these conclusions independently.

What Can We Do About It?

Living with the mindset that men are dense is neither healthy nor reality. Remember—the particular gifts and strengths of men and women are complementary, but they are not exclusive to one gender or the other. God calls both men and women to help each other cultivate the unique gifts which they are "the reminder and the privileged sign of." [71]

To help accomplish this with the gift of intuition, one thing women can do is allow men to take more ownership of certain situations and lead. Of course, women *can* lead and there is a place for women in leadership, but if women do not want to be continually dragging men along in relationships, parenthood, the office, and so forth, they need to give them the opportunity to exercise their intuition.

A mom sometimes needs to let dad be dad, even if he does not do it the "right" way. A girlfriend sometimes needs to challenge a boyfriend to step it up, and if he does not, she might need to walk away. Instead of telling the men in their lives what to do, women sometimes need to share their perspectives and then allow them to use their intuition to decide on their own. [72]

---

71 Ratzinger and Amato, 14.
72 If there is a moral issue that sends one, or both of you, to the sacrament of Reconciliation, change needs to happen immediately.

This was an approach that Catherine brilliantly used when Pope Gregory XI was having second thoughts about leaving Avignon. She encouragingly wrote to him:

> Now is the time to give your life for the little sheep who have left the flock. You must seek and win them back by using patience ... I am confident that by God's measureless goodness you will win back the unbelievers ...
>
> Don't be surprised even though you see a great deal of opposition, and see that human help is failing us, and that those who should be helping us most disappoint us and act against us. Don't be afraid, but even more self-confident; don't give up or restrain your sweet holy desire, but let it be more enkindled with each day that passes.
>
> Up, father! Put into effect the resolution you have made concerning your return ...
>
> Have a courageous, absolutely fearless heart, as you follow the Lamb who was slain and consumed on the cross for us! Keep living in God's holy and tender love. Please, reverend father, grant the request that Neri, the bearer of this letter, will communicate to you, if you find it possible and acceptable.[73]

In the letter, Catherine led with humility and did not nag or belittle the pope. She did not try to manipulate him to do the right thing. She told him to have courage. She told him she believed in him— and she asked him to take her request into consideration.

This letter is a beautiful example of how women can live out one of St. John Paul II's insights on intuition. In *Redemptoris Mater*, he writes, "The Church sees in the face of women ... the ability to combine penetrating intuition with words of support and encouragement."[74] Sometimes, our intuition is best used to support and encourage, not to boss others around.

73 Catherine of Siena, *The Letters of St. Catherine of Siena: Volume 1*, 229–232.
74 John Paul II, *Redemptoris Mater* (March 25, 1987), 46, vatican.va.

Intuition Challenge

This chapter's challenge is to write a letter to someone in your life whom you know needs some encouragement. Combine your penetrating intuition with words of support and encouragement (and don't forget a big dose of humility!). Like Catherine did for Pope Gregory XI, tell the person who receives your letter to have courage, tell him you believe in him, and if you offer any advice, invite him to take what you have said into consideration.

Discussion Questions

1. Do you identify with the gift of intuition? Why or why not? What factors in your life have either stifled or encouraged growth in this gift?

2. Do you agree with the assessment that intuition is when you *just know?* When in your life has this feminine intuition proved valuable?

3. When have you seen the influence of women in "all spheres of society" prove to be valuable in humanizing a situation? Perhaps in politics, the Church, a school, or the workplace?

4. What did you find most inspiring about the life of St. Catherine of Siena? What lessons on the feminine genius gift of intuition can you learn from her?

5. Have you ever dragged someone along in a relationship, romantic or otherwise? What was the experience like? Did anything change to improve things?

6. What is one way that you can reveal the gift of intuition to your family, friends, community, or world?

CHAPTER 7

Generosity and Servant of God Julia Greeley

For eleven years, Kevin and I fundraised our salary. As we worked as missionaries, we mainly relied on the generosity of others to feed, clothe, and shelter our growing family. However, soon after we began our work, we almost had to walk away. Our funding was short by $1,800 per month, so we begged the Lord to send more mission partners and fast. One way he responded was by connecting us with a military wife. She invited Kevin to speak at her local Catholic mom's group that met at her base's interdenominational chapel. Kevin had recently done a pitch like this for a men's group. Not a single person stepped up to join us. I thought, somewhat sarcastically, *Great, Lord, a mom's group. This will be so fruitful.* I suggested that the event might be a waste of time, but Kevin showed up and faithfully gave his presentation. Afterward, a steady flow of women approached to thank him for his time ... and to hand him a commitment card. In the end, ten women from the small group joined our support team on a monthly basis.

Over the years, the generosity of these women continued to surprise us. They invited me to join their mom's group.

These women—whose husbands were deployed—offered to babysit *my* kids so I could have some time to myself. They made treat bags for our students going on the long bus ride to our annual FOCUS conference. Even after we moved, they added us to their Christmas card lists and sent gifts when we had a new baby. I often think about these selfless women who so beautifully revealed the gift of feminine generosity to me. They will forever be some of my personal heroes. After all, they are the ones who tipped the scales so we could spend nine more years serving as FOCUS missionaries.

Making Room for Generosity

We all have our own experiences with the generosity of women in our lives. Maybe at your aunt's house there was always room for one more at the dinner table. Perhaps you had a teacher who seemed to go above and beyond for her students. Or there was that youth minister who never turned down a chance to meet you for coffee when you needed a listening ear.

While personal experience alone certainly reveals the generosity of women, hard data does as well. A quick online search on the differences between men's and women's volunteer habits brings up study after study indicating that women consistently outdo men in volunteer hours. One could speculate that the numbers reveal a gap because of stay-at-home moms, but taking care of children full-time does not leave much free time for volunteering outside of the home. Yet, with or without stay-at-home moms, research proves that "no matter the income level, age or working status, women are more likely to volunteer."[75]

When you add personal experience with research findings, it is easy to see why St. John Paul II wrote in his *Letter to Women,*

---

75 Dan Kopf, "Why Don't Men Volunteer as Much as Women?," *Priceonomics,* December, 17, 2015, priceonomics.com/.

"Women are ever ready and willing to give themselves generously to others, especially in serving the weakest and most defenseless."[76] For John Paul II, this feminine generosity is a fundamental part of who a woman is because it flows from her receptive and maternal nature. A woman's "capacity for the other,"[77] in the words of Pope Benedict XVI, gives her a penchant to make space for others. Here again, the visible reveals the invisible. Not only does a woman have a physical capacity for another through pregnancy, but she also has a spiritual capacity for another through her gift of self. She makes space for others at her table, on her calendar, and in her heart. In so many circumstances, women offer themselves in ways that necessitate a large dose of generosity.

It Doesn't *Feel* Like Generosity

However, for many women, their acts of generosity do not *feel* generous, so they don't think much of them. Ask any pregnant woman if she pats herself on the back each night, saying, "Wow, I am so generous for allowing this baby to take up residence inside of me." Or ask a woman who rearranged her schedule to make time for a friend in need, or babysat her grandkids so her daughter could get away with her husband, or took on the extra load at work—ask her if she is generous, and she will likely just shrug her shoulders.

So often, women fail to see their heroic acts as generous because they seem so ordinary. Millions of women make seemingly insignificant sacrifices for others daily. These acts are rarely grandiose and seem menial when you compare them to a million-dollar check to build a hospital in a developing country. Yet generosity is so much more than grand gestures memorialized with plaques in lobbies or awards presented at fundraising galas. The everyday generosity that women freely give without counting

---

76   John Paul II, *Letter to Women,* 8.

77   Ratzinger and Amato, 13.

the cost is true, heroic generosity.

When thinking of a saint to uphold as an example of feminine genius generosity, the first person who came to mind was St. Teresa of Calcutta, who gave her entire life to serving the poorest of the poor. However, most of us know and love her already. Instead, I am turning to my hometown hero Julia Greeley, a woman many of us do not yet know but who is on the path to sainthood.

Meet Servant of God Julia Greeley

In 2016, the cause for canonization of Denver's "Angel of Charity," Julia Greeley, was officially opened. While I had heard of her life and witness, I had not visited any holy sites associated with her or her work. So, after dropping my three "big kids" off at school one morning, my toddler and I went on a pilgrimage. Unlike my St. Catherine of Siena journey, we did not have to fly to Europe to visit the church, home, and tomb of a Catholic hero. Instead, we made the rounds using our minivan and were home by lunchtime.

To start, my pint-sized companion and I began our day at Julia's home parish, Sacred Heart. Built in 1880, the largely untouched church is a step back in time. As I took in the space filled with sacred images and holy statues that Julia would have contemplated more than a hundred years ago, I could not help but feel her presence.

From there, we followed in Julia's footsteps as we walked the streets outside of Sacred Heart looking at buildings she visited and lived in before heading to Julia's final resting place at the Cathedral Basilica of the Immaculate Conception. Prominently placed to the left of the altar is Julia's white marble tomb. Remarkably, it is the only tomb in the whole of the sanctuary. For as long as my toddler would allow, I knelt and prayed for Julia's intercession before beginning to write her story for this book.[78]

---

78 As a side note, if you have saints (or prospective saints) from your area, I recommend getting to know them. If you do not know of any, call your diocesan chancery office and inquire—you might be surprised.

Finding Faith

Retelling the life of Julia Greeley is a challenge. Born into slavery and freed through the Emancipation Ordinance of Missouri in 1865, Julia could barely read and never learned how to write.[79] Her lack of education means that there are no writings of Julia and very few recordings of her words. Even her exact birth date is unknown (even to her); historians have estimated it to be between 1833 and 1848. What we do know of Julia's early life is that she was likely born at the Samuel B. Caldwell plantation near Hannibal, Missouri, and, when she was too young to remember, she lost her right eye to the whip of a cruel slave master who was abusing her mother.

Before leaving Missouri, Julia spent her final decade in slavery as a cook and nanny for the Robinson family in St. Louis. Lina Robinson introduced Julia to her sister, who was also named Julia. This Julia eventually married the first territorial governor of Colorado, Colonel William Gilpin. Sometime between 1878 and 1880, Julia Greeley made her way to Denver, where the Gilpin's employed her as a household servant.

Julia Gilpin, who had attended St. Joseph Academy in Emmitsburg, Maryland (founded by St. Elizabeth Ann Seton), introduced Julia Greeley to the Catholic Faith. Julia's faith deepened quickly, and she formally entered the Church shortly after her arrival in Denver. She was baptized on June 26, 1880, a few months after the dedication of Sacred Heart Church.

As time passed, Julia Gilpin and Julia Greeley developed a unique bond. When Julia finished her work at the end of each day, she would sit on the floor in Mrs. Gilpin's room and chat with her about the family and children. Unfortunately, there was strife in the Gilpin marriage, and, despite Mrs. Gilpin's liking of Julia,

---

79 Blaine Burkey, *In Secret Service of the Sacred Heart: The Life and Virtues of Julia Greeley* (Denver, CO: Julia Greeley Guild, 2012), 104.

Colonel Gilpin formed a strong prejudice against her. As a way to "annoy and wound" his wife, he discharged Julia from their employ in 1883.[80] He also spread vicious rumors about Julia's character that played into racial stereotypes that were prevalent at the time, making it difficult for her to find work. While Mrs. Gilpin tried to help Julia find work, each position she secured never lasted for long. Over the next five years, Julia moved around Colorado, Wyoming, and New Mexico to accept whatever work she could find.

In 1887, Colonel Gilpin filed for divorce from Mrs. Gilpin.[81] He listed twenty-four complaints against her, the fourteenth of which declared that she threatened his household's morality with the presence of the "lewd and unprincipled" Julia Greeley.[82] A subpoena brought Julia back to Denver to testify on Mrs. Gilpin's behalf. Other witnesses contradicted Colonel Gilpin's false accusations, and in the end, the trial exonerated Julia. She remained in the area from then on. Despite the struggles that resulted from her defamation, Julia remained faithful to Mrs. Gilpin. When people told her that the family ought to leave her a little money, she would reply, "They've given me more than money—they gave me my faith."[83]

Living Faith

Thanks to the trial, we know more about Julia's life in the 1880s than of any other decade. Her later years can only be pieced together through censuses, Church records, newspaper articles, and personal testimonies. From these sources, it is known that Julia continued to work domestic jobs around Denver, and when

80 Burkey, 84.
81 Colonel Gilpin won the case, but Mrs. Gilpin appealed the ruling to the Colorado Supreme Court. At the Supreme Court the ruling was overturned. In 1891, the Gilpins reconciled and once again lived as husband and wife.
82 Burkey, 76.
83 Burkey, 55.

she could not find consistent work, she picked up odd jobs as a day laborer. Additionally, she remained a devout Catholic whose love of the Faith was apparent to all.

Julia began each day with Mass, calling the Eucharist her "breakfast." In 1901, she became a member of the Third Order of St. Francis, choosing the name Elizabeth, after St. Elizabeth of Hungary, who spent her life serving the poor in as much secrecy as possible. As an active member of her parish's Sacred Heart League, Julia walked to each Denver fire station every month to pass out red rosaries, Sacred Heart badges, and leaflets that promoted devotion to the Sacred Heart of Jesus. Knowing the dangerous work of firefighters, she wanted to ensure that these brave men knew Jesus and were prepared for their death at any moment.

Always filled with joy and a sense of fun, Julia held a particular love for children and remained childlike herself. At night, when children were out playing, Julia often joined them to "sing and dance and laugh."[84] She was a favorite when it came time for choosing a Confirmation sponsor, and in her free time, she gathered children for trolley rides and picnics. Once, when the young girls of her parish organized a beauty contest, Julia, advanced in years and missing an eye, convinced her firefighter friends to buy ten-cent tickets to vote for her. She swept the contest raising $350.00—that is, selling a whopping 3,500 tickets!

Despite Julia's fun-loving disposition and devotion to her faith, the racism of the time cast a shadow on her efforts to practice the Faith. For Mass, Julia rented a front-row pew on the left side of the sanctuary, which kept her segregated from white parishioners. Nonetheless, some complained, saying Julia should not sit in the front row for Mass with her floppy, "hand-me-down" clothes. When Julia heard this, she told the pastor she could attend another

---

84 Burkey, 50.

Mass, but he replied, "Julia, you're going to keep your regular seat and come to high Mass like you always do, because I know you want to. Julia can sit any place in this church she wants to."[85]

Fulfilling Faith

As a devotee to the Sacred Heart, Julia would have looked forward to Friday, June 7, 1918. That year, the seventh of June was nineteen days after Pentecost, making it the Solemnity of the Sacred Heart of Jesus. Of course, as with all first Fridays of the month, it was already a day dedicated to the Sacred Heart, a tradition that dates to the seventeenth century when Jesus appeared to St. Margaret Mary Alacoque. The Lord promised her particular graces for whoever said special prayers and engaged in devotions to the Sacred Heart on the first Friday of the month. These promises include the grace of his divine Heart being an assured refuge at a devotee's final moment on earth.

That morning, which was doubly set apart for the Sacred Heart, Julia headed to Sacred Heart Church for daily Mass. On the way, she fell gravely ill. A priest was called to administer last rites, and shortly after, Julia was taken to St. Joseph's Hospital. Hours later, one can hardly doubt that the Sacred Heart of Jesus came to comfort Julia in her final moments, as he had promised.

Following Julia's passing, the *Denver Post* issued an ordinary notice regarding her funeral arrangements but omitted details of her wake. Nonetheless, when Julia's viewing began at Loyola Chapel, crowds lined the streets to pay their respects. Hundreds of mourners of every age, status, and race steadily flowed through the chapel for five straight hours. Love for Julia poured in from all corners of the city, and articles about her began to fill the local papers.

But why? Why was there such an outpouring of love for this

---

85 Burkey, 50.

uneducated, marginalized woman who struggled to find stable work? Why is she now buried in a cathedral with the title "Servant of God"? It is not because of her spiritual writings; there are none. She did not found a religious community or levitate or die a martyr. *What she did was generously love.*

Revealing the Gift of Generosity

It was only after Julia's death that Denverites discovered that everyone seemed to have a story about "Old Julia."[86] Many knew of her love of neighbor and generosity, but it was not until her passing that the depth of her giving heart was finally revealed. For decades, in the cover of darkness, Julia roamed her neighborhood giving in secret, just like her Confirmation namesake, St. Elizabeth of Hungary. Knowing her neighbors would be embarrassed to receive assistance from her, she kept her aid secret.

Pulling a red wagon or carrying a knapsack, Julia delivered items that she collected by spending from her meager wages, begging on behalf of others, or giving away gifts intended for her. Clothes, food, and household items frequently came in and out of her hands as Julia attentively watched and took mental notes on others' needs.

One cold night, Julia left a sack of potatoes on the front porch of a needy family. Fearing the potatoes would freeze, she stayed to make sure someone brought them in. When nobody came to the door, she sent a neighborhood boy to knock and run away. If anyone asked, she instructed him, "Don't you dare say Old Julia sent you!"[87] Another time, when young girls in her parish were not coming to youth activities because they could not afford appropriate dresses, Julia went to an affluent part of town and asked the wealthy

---

86 Unfortunately, due to racial discrimination, Julia had many other nicknames that are not worth printing here.

87 Blaine Burkey, *An Hour with Julia Greeley* (Liguori, MO: Liguori Publications, 2020), 16.

families to buy new dresses for their daughters so that she could pass their gently used dresses on to "her girls."[88] This arrangement soon became a common exchange, as Julia convinced them that their daughters needed new dresses on a regular basis.

Further accounts tell of Julia finding and delivering baby buggies to pregnant mothers, carrying a mattress on her back in a dark alley at night, and supplying funeral clothes and food whenever a family was in mourning. Once, she even gave up her grave for a deceased elderly black man to prevent him from being buried in a potter's field. Julia's generosity truly knew no limits. For her, finding ways to provide for others flowed from her trust in Jesus' providence, and giving was a privilege and a joy. As a reporter once put it, "She never thought of her deeds as 'charity.' She had friends who never failed her. The Sacred Heart and St. Anthony would show her the way."[89]

How Can Generosity Get Twisted?

As Julia's life attests, women possess a rich ability to be generous. Because of their capacity for others, they tend to see their needs—and, out of the generosity of their hearts, they find ways to meet them. Women want to live generously. However, possessing this gift does not mean that they always choose to live from it, especially when fear holds them back.

It can be easy to fear being generous. Continually giving away one's time, money, energy, or emotions can lead to a shortage of these finite resources. While this is a reasonable concern, we need to ensure that this fear of running out does not prevent us from trusting that the Lord will provide.

If anyone knew how to conquer this fear of scarcity, it was Julia.

88   Burkey, *In the Secret Service of the Sacred Heart*, 28.
89   Burkey, 28.

She gave everything to the Lord. Her time, money, shelter, work—her very self—was entrusted to the Sacred Heart of Jesus, and she knew God would provide. Even when finding work was a day-by-day task, she still spent her nights giving in secret, sometimes from items that others had given to her that day. As one testimony shared, "If you gave her an apple or an orange or candy it went into the bag, and somebody got it at the next house she visited."[90] Julia lived generously because she never feared that God would forget to provide.

Another fear that can hold us back from being generous is a fear of rejection. A generous exchange involves a certain level of vulnerability on the part of both giver and receiver. In offering to give and in asking to receive, either party can reject the other's offer. We have all experienced the pain of rejection, so it seems safer to hold back from being generous and keep to ourselves in times of need. Unfortunately, this is all too easy to do because people do not seem to really need each other anymore.

In the past, generous giving and receiving was a necessity. For thousands of years, people depended on each other for survival. But now it is easy to live isolated, individualistic lives that require little to no help from others. Why ask a friend to bring over a post-surgery meal or medical supplies when a delivery service can drop them by? Why ask for help when trying to solve a problem when you can figure it out by doing an Internet search or watching a video tutorial? While it is easy to find ways to take care of ourselves without bothering anybody, this approach negates opportunities for us and others to live generously.

Julia was able to be generous because she knew the needs of her community. She knew which girls were skipping social events because she passed out the punch at the event's refreshment table.

---

90 Burkey, 59.

She noticed which families were struggling to buy food or who needed a mattress because she frequently visited her neighbors' homes. Julia knew God did not create people for isolation. She knew that as the body of Christ, we belong to each other, and it is our responsibility to take care of each other.

What Can We Do About It?

Fears about generosity are notorious for holding people back from doing what they know they ought to do. When it comes to scarcity, perhaps you know you should be tithing to your church or donating to a cause, but you are afraid of how that might impact your savings account. Or maybe you know God desires for you to give generously of your time to a project or ministry, but you are worried that it will prevent you from keeping up with your to-do list. The fear of running out can paralyze us in many ways, yet I have found that the best way to overcome this fear is to challenge it. Be generous and see how he provides.

But what if the fear that holds you back is not a fear of scarcity but of rejection. Perhaps you are worried that if you step out in faith and offer your time to a project or reach out to a hurting friend, he or she may not want your generosity? This could happen. There were times when people rejected Julia's generosity, which likely attributed to her giving under cover of darkness. But this rejection did not stop her, and it should not stop you. If God is calling you to be generous, do not let fear hold you back. Reveal the gift. Our broken world needs your generosity. It needs a reminder that we belong to each other.

Generosity Challenge

For this chapter's challenge, I invite you to find an intentional way to be generous with someone this week. We all know the stories of someone paying for coffee for the person behind them at the drive-through window. While this is good, it is not what I am suggesting here. Instead of helping out a stranger, consider being generous to someone close to you.

Why? Because the goal here is not to feel satisfied over a random act of kindness but to be generous in a way that requires vulnerability. As St. Teresa of Calcutta, who took care of strangers every day, wisely said, "It is easy to love the people far away … It is not always easy to love those close to us. It is easier to give a cup of rice to relieve hunger than to relieve the loneliness and pain of someone unloved in our own home."[91]

Maybe you have a classmate or coworker who is struggling to find community, and you could be generous in sharing your friends with them. Maybe you have a spouse who needs support in a way that requires you to draw strength from the Lord to find the emotional energy to be there for him. Maybe it is the Lord himself who you need to be generous with as he asks you to be open to him in ways that make you nervous. Whatever it is, be generous in a way that reminds others that we belong to each other—and that nobody is ever alone.

---

91   David Scott, *The Love That Made Mother Teresa* (Manchester, NH: Sophia Institute Press, 2013), 48.

Discussion Questions

1. Can you identify with the gift of generosity? Why or why not? What factors in your life have either stifled or encouraged growth in this gift?

2. In what ways have you experienced the generosity of women in your life?

3. Does the idea that women do not recognize their natural generosity as true generosity resonate with you? Why or why not?

4. What did you find most inspiring about the life of Servant of God Julia Greeley? What lessons about the feminine genius gift of generosity can you learn from her?

5. How have generosity fears effected your giving in the past? Do you tend to struggle more with the fear of scarcity or the fear of rejection?

6. What is one way that you can reveal the gift of generosity to your family, friends, community, or world?

CHAPTER 8

Fidelity and the Women at the Cross

In the early sixteenth century, the Protestant Reformation shook the foundations of many Catholic countries in Europe. While many felt the impact, women religious in particular took a blow because, according to Protestantism, marriage was the only proper state for women. This belief created an interesting predicament for the Reformers: What would they do with all the single nuns?

Some areas sought to deal with the problem by offering women religious a sort of "severance package" for quitting their vocation as a bride of Christ. The deal included a pension and help in finding a husband, usually from the pool of former monks and priests.[92] Since it was not uncommon for women to be forced into the convent at this time in history, some happily welcomed this offer of liberation. Most consecrated women, though, had freely chosen to take religious vows and loved their vocation. Some were forced out of their convents and had to find alternative ways to live their vocation, while others staunchly refused to leave their communal homes and responded with active resistance.

---

92 Amy Leonard, *Nails in the Wall: Catholic Nuns in Reformation Germany* (Chicago: The University of Chicago Press, 2005), 6.

Perplexed over why these women would not want to abandon a "corrupt" religion, some Protestant leaders had to find creative ways to eradicate female religious. For some, this meant the forcible relocation of communities to areas that were still Catholic. For others, it meant forbidding religious communities from accepting new members. And for those who still believed converting nuns was possible, it meant implementing a reeducation program that replaced Catholic priests with Protestant pastors.

With no choice but to fight back, faithful sisters became equally creative in their goal of maintaining communal life as brides of Christ. Relocated communities left with plans to one day return. Communities who had been forbidden to admit new members cleverly argued that their services were vital as civic institutions. As for those who were forced to listen to Protestant preaching, well, in one case, the sisters used their cloistered life to their advantage.

Because cloistered nuns live apart from the world, visitors can only be with them from behind a screen. Knowing that their assigned Protestant pastor would only see shadows behind this screen, the Dominican sisters at the convents of Saints Margaret and Agnes in Strasbourg, Germany put habits on statues and placed them where they were supposed to sit during services. Then elderly sisters, who were hard of hearing and firm in their beliefs, sat among the statues and occasionally shuffled around to give the illusion of an audience.[93] The ruse worked for months before an enthusiastic preacher knocked the screen over and discovered the deception.

While it certainly would have been easier for these nuns to go along with the changes of their time, nothing could entice them to abandon their vocations. Their fidelity was unshakable, and when the Catholic Faith was restored in their area, small but steadfast

---

93 Leonard, 80.

bands of sisters either went back home or had remained there to welcome its return.

Limitless

I love the stories of sisters who fought to maintain the Faith during the Protestant Reformation. Despite challenging circumstances, they remained unwaveringly faithful to both their Spouse and fellow sisters in their communities. While the actions of these women were certainly noteworthy, they were likely not surprising to St. John Paul II, who not only thanked women for their fidelity in his *Letter to Women*,[94] but also praised them for this fidelity being "limitless" in his encyclical *Redemptoris Mater*.[95]

As part of their person-oriented feminine genius, women tend to be particularly devoted to both their God and their people. When it comes to God, statistics repeatedly show that more women than men say religion is "very important" in their lives, which is likely why more women than men pray daily and attend religious services weekly.[96] Even during the Protestant Reformation, women's resolute fidelity shined as female religious communities outnumbered their male counterparts in terms of survival rate.[97] While history and statistics back up John Paul II's insights, this is likely your personal experience as it seems everybody knows several spectacular single Catholic women who are struggling to find an equally spectacular single Catholic guy.

Still, demonstrations of a woman's fidelity are not only apparent in how she devotes herself to God but also in how she devotes herself to others. Here again, it is easy to find data highlighting

---

94 John Paul II, *Letter to Women*, 2.

95 John Paul II, *Redemptoris Mater*, 46.

96 "The Gender Gap in Religion Around the World," Pew Research Center, March 22, 2016, pewforum.org/.

97 Leonard, 5.

this tendency as statistics repeatedly indicate that women are less likely to cheat in committed relationships.

All of this points to the reality that when a woman connects herself to someone—be it a child, family member, sweetheart, friend, or God—she does not easily let go. This gift allows her not to give up on someone, even when they have given up on themselves. It motivates her not to run away when things get hard, but instead fight for the relationship. It also gives her the strength to stand by somebody, even when that means taking a risk.

The women of the Reformation demonstrated this type of fidelity as they stood by their Lord despite persecution. In doing so, they were like the faithful band of women who originally stood by Jesus' side at his crucifixion. These women at the Cross, who remained with Our Lord during his final hours, are one of the most remarkable examples of limitless fidelity.

Meet the Women at the Cross

Women are hardly even mentioned in the first fourteen chapters of the Gospel of Mark. In the fifteenth chapter, though, a dramatic shift occurs. When Jesus is condemned to death and picks up his cross, the leading male characters are replaced with previously unmentioned female characters. What accounts for this sudden shift? Women take center stage because the apostles, except for John, go missing. Out of fear, they are hiding from everything happening around Calvary—and in the process, they miss Jesus' crucifixion, death, burial, and resurrection.

While the apostles were missing in action, however, Jesus' faithful female followers were present. They did not hide; instead, they remained by his side and witnessed it all. As St. John Paul II admiringly writes, "As we see, in this most arduous test of faith and fidelity, the women proved stronger than the Apostles. In this moment of danger, those who love much succeed in overcoming their fear."[98] The women stayed, watched, and witnessed.

This is an incredible detail. Through the Holy Spirit's inspiration, men wrote the Gospel accounts of Jesus' final days. But because they were not there to witness it, they got their information from the firsthand accounts of women. If it were not for these women's fidelity, much less would be known from eyewitness accounts about what happened when the Son of God saved the world.

Jesus' Female Followers

The women at the Cross are so important to salvation history that Mark's Gospel is not the only one to highlight the presence of Jesus' faithful female followers. All four Gospels, as well as the Stations of the Cross, emphasize the presence of women during Jesus' crucifixion, burial, and resurrection because the existence of these women matter—they were the primary witnesses of these events. While we can know little of their personal lives, their actions speak volumes about their fidelity.

In the Stations of the Cross, the presence of women notably defines three of the fourteen points of meditation. Firstly, at the fourth station, Jesus meets his mother, Mary. She was with her Son from the moment of his conception, and Scripture attests that she faithfully remained with him until his very end. Her Son returns her fidelity, as one of his final actions on the Cross was entrusting Mary to the Beloved Apostle John (see John 19:25-27).

At the sixth station, Veronica wipes the face of Jesus. While this scene is not noted in any of the Gospel accounts, tradition holds that Veronica was the hemorrhaging woman healed by touching the hem of Jesus' garment (see Matthew 9:20-22), which took place right after Jesus calls Matthew to be an apostle. This detail

---

98 John Paul II, *Mulieris Dignitatem*, 15.

reveals that, if she was indeed the woman with the hemorrhage, Veronica's first encounter with Jesus took place in Galilee during the early days of his public ministry. So perhaps Veronica was in Jerusalem simply because it was Passover, or perhaps she had traveled to the Holy City just to be with Jesus in his final hours.

Finally, at the eighth station, Jesus meets the weeping women of Jerusalem, telling them not to cry for him but for themselves and their children (see Luke 23:27-31). Nothing more is known of these women, but their influence was significant enough to warrant a moment of pause each time someone prays the Stations of the Cross.

While the Stations of the Cross clearly demonstrate the presence of women along the way to Calvary, we learn even more about the other women who were at the Cross through Scripture. Surrounding Jesus' crucifixion, death, and resurrection, each Gospel notes the presence of women, explicitly naming some individuals.

The Gospel writers list some women by name because they were their eyewitnesses who give credibility to the events depicted. Many Catholic scholars agree that five women are identified by name as witnesses to Jesus' crucifixion. What makes this number challenging to nail down is that many of them are named Mary. Of course, we know one was Jesus' mother, but who were the other four women at the foot of the Cross?

First, all four Gospels mention the presence of Mary Magdalene. This Mary clearly plays a leading role as a female follower as she is the first person Jesus appears to after his resurrection (see Mark 16:9; John 20:11-18). Like Veronica, Mary Magdalene's relationship with Jesus goes back to Galilee when he cast out seven demons from her (see Luke 8:2). While she is not mentioned again until the Cross, Luke makes it clear that from the time of her healing, Mary Magdalene, along with a handful of other women, traveled with Jesus and his twelve apostles.

Next is Mary, the mother of James the younger and Joseph (or Joses). Before including this Mary as a witness at Calvary, the Gospel of Mark introduced her sons when Jesus was visiting Nazareth. In the scene, Mark refers to James and Joseph as Jesus' brothers (see Mark 6:3), which is a bit confusing in English, given the perpetual virginity of the Blessed Mother. The Greek word translated "brother" here, *adelphos*, was used for siblings, cousins, other blood relatives, or even a covenant relationship. Given the expansive meaning of this term, scholars believe that Mary and her two sons were relatives of Jesus.

One final point of clarification on this confusing Mary, who in Matthew's account is also sometimes referred to as "the other Mary": her son "James the younger" is not St. James the apostle, whose mother, Salome, was another witness of the Crucifixion.

The Gospels of Matthew and Mark both list Salome as a witness at the Cross, but they give her different titles. Mark calls her by her name, Salome, and Matthew calls her "the mother of the sons of Zebedee" (see Matthew 27:56). This makes Salome the wife of Zebedee and the apostles James and John's mother—as in John, the only apostle present at the Cross. It also makes Salome the bold mother who asked Jesus to command her sons to sit at his right and his left in his kingdom—that is, "Please make them powerful." Given her past boldness, it is likely that Salome was a disciple of Jesus along with her sons, or she at least knew him reasonably well because of her sons' relationship with him.

The final witness named in the Gospels is Joanna. While Luke only records her presence at the Resurrection, it is likely she would have witnessed Jesus' death and burial as well. Twice in his Passion account, Luke refers to "the women who had followed him from Galilee" (see Luke 23:49, 55). Joanna was likely one of these women because Luke 8:2-3 tells us that in Galilee, Jesus cured Joanna and, like Mary Magdalene, after that moment, she followed him.

Revealing the Gift of Fidelity

The women named at the Cross represented many of Jesus' first female followers. Some, like his Mother Mary and likely Mary the mother of James the younger and Joseph, were family members. Some, like Salome, were family members of apostles. Some, like Veronica, Joanna, and Mary Magdalene, were among those who knew the healing power of Jesus. Each of the three synoptic Gospels is careful to point out that these women—many of whom had been with Jesus since the beginning of his public ministry—"followed" Jesus (see Matthew 27:55; Mark 15:41; Luke 23:49, 55) and "provided for" or "ministered to" him (see Matthew 27:55; Mark 15:41; Luke 8:3).[99] Paying attention to these word choices is important because they tell us that Jesus' female followers were more than just "fans" of him; rather, they were true and faithful disciples.

The same Greek word used to describe the way the disciples Peter and Andrew "followed" Jesus, or the way James and John "followed" Jesus, is used to describe the way the women "followed" Jesus (see Matthew 4:20 and Luke 5:11). The Gospel writers use this same word each time to show that the women were true disciples who were as committed as the men.

When the Gospel writers describe how the women "provided for" Jesus or "ministered to" him, they use the same Greek word used for Jesus' mission of service (see Mark 10:45). With these phrases, we see that the women were faithful disciples who imitated Jesus by ministering to him materially while he cared for them spiritually.

These women's material services likely included humble tasks such as making Jesus' meals or washing his clothes and providing for his mission out of their own financial resources (see Luke 8:3). However, their providing for him would have also gone well

---

99 The synoptic Gospels are Matthew, Mark, and Luke, which follow a similar chronology and contain similar episodes in the life of Jesus.

beyond domestic chores and money. In addition, they would have provided him with friendship and moral support, which is evident in how they accompanied him on the way of the Cross.

When all others abandoned Jesus, the presence of his faithful female disciples would have been the primary source of support extended to him during his passion. They were there for him despite the danger. They were there for him despite the emotional agony it must have caused them. Can you imagine actually witnessing Jesus' passion and crucifixion? It must have been heart-wrenching, yet these women were there because they loved him. Out of gratitude for all he had done for them—the ways he ministered to them and healed them both physically and spiritually—they used their feminine genius gift of fidelity to remain by his side.

How Can Fidelity Get Twisted?

Jesus' first female disciples give us a beautiful image of what it means to live feminine genius fidelity. A woman's inclination to be faithful, even in the toughest of situations, is a true gift, but like with each of the feminine genius gifts, it can get twisted if not properly directed.

Sticking by people is what women do. This tendency to be faithful to those they love and care about is a good thing. However, problems can arise when this desire to remain faithful keeps them in unhealthy relationships or wrong situations.

Each of us has witnessed this: The family member who puts up with a manipulative friendship because she would feel bad for abandoning it; the classmate who knows she has no time to volunteer with a particular organization but cannot bring herself to quit because she does not want to let everyone down; the friend who refuses to put boundaries around a toxic work situation because she is still holding out for people to change.

In each of these situations, walking away can be tricky because everything inside a woman does not want to give up on a person, project, or commitment. Her faithful heart desires to support and help. As a result, she sticks around, even if it is time to set boundaries or let go altogether.

The Emotions

One reason for this unwavering devotion is that there are many emotions involved in circumstances tied to people. While emotions are natural, if the intellect and will do not correctly guide them, they can easily blind us to the reality of a situation.

The chapter on self-giving addressed the concept of the intellect and will. As a reminder, our intellect gives us the ability to think and reason, and our will gives us the ability to choose an action. When these two "faculties" (or abilities) are working together, they help us to make sound decisions—unless our passions get in the way.

Passions are our physical and emotional desires. They cause us to experience feelings, which are objectively neither right nor wrong; they simply *are*. Emotions are not a conscious choice but simply happen to come upon us, so they are morally neutral. What matters is what we choose to do with them. In other words, our actions are what matter. As the *Catechism of the Catholic Church* says, "Emotions and feelings can be taken up in the virtues or perverted by the vices."[100] This means that emotions can either be used in a positive way, or they can get twisted and be used in a negative way.

As we have seen, it is not uncommon for there to be many different emotions tied to fidelity. This is especially true for women, who are inclined to "see persons with their hearts."[101] This gift allows women to create emotional bonds with people, which is a good

---

100 CCC 1774.

101 John Paul II, *Letter to Women*, 12.

thing—except when such bonds need to be broken.

Imagine a couple who have been dating for about a year. When they started their relationship, they were both pretty neutral about their faith. Still, they tried to get to Mass on Sundays, and they genuinely wanted to be good people who did the right thing. However, as time went on, the woman started to grow closer to Jesus, and being Catholic took on new importance in her life. At the same time, her boyfriend began to drift away from his faith, and it became less and less of a priority to him. These changes caused the gap in their faith lives to grow so big that the woman soon realized their relationship was not headed in the direction she wanted. At the same time, she was terrified of what might happen if they broke up.

What if he is the one, and I blow it? she begins to think. *What if we break up and nobody else is there to bring Jesus into his life? We have been through so much together. How could I possibly just walk away from it all? Maybe he will change?* While all of these objections for staying together swirled around in her head, deep down she knew the relationship was not right.

What Can We Do About It?

Here is where the need for the intellect and will to properly guide and direct the emotions comes into play. The emotions are neither rational nor reasonable, yet we often allow them to be the determining factor in decision making. For example, the woman we just considered knew what she needed to do, but her emotions—which told her to hang on and be faithful—prevented her from doing it. Her natural desire to remain faithful to her boyfriend was not objectively bad. However, what was mainly guiding her were her emotions, and she refused to allow her intellect to engage her decision making. Unfortunately, this tendency is common, but becoming aware of it can go a long way in preventing the emotions from taking advantage of faithful hearts.

One thing you can do to prevent the emotions from twisting your faithful heart is to allow your reason to have a say in decision making. Again, this is not to say that the emotions have no place in discernment, but allowing them to be the driving force can lead to poor decisions. Taking time to intentionally consider life choices is critical in every stage of life. Simple steps like praying about who and what you chose to be faithful to, seeking counsel from others, and asking yourself tough questions about the reality of a situation can go a long way.

If you want to know what can happen when the intellect is allowed to properly order the emotions, just look to the women at the foot of the Cross. We can imagine that their emotions were mixed with fear and anxiety along with love and compassion. If they had allowed fear to control them, they would have been in hiding, far away from Jesus. Instead, as John Paul II points out, "Those who love much succeed in overcoming their fear."[102] Their intellect told them, "Your friend needs you, get over your fear and be there for him!" Fortunately, they chose to listen, and they did the right thing.

Fidelity Challenge

For this chapter's challenge, I invite you to examine who you are, or are not, faithful to and ask why. To start, write down a list of any persons or groups of people to whom you are faithful to. This list might include God, family members, your husband (if you are married), a boyfriend (if you are dating), friends, coworkers, a church community, or a volunteer community. Then look at the list and add any persons or groups of people that you *should be* faithful to.

Then, look at each individual or group and ask yourself whether your fidelity to them is ordered rightly, or if your emotions are causing your fidelity to be disorder. Keep in mind this question

---

102 John Paul II, *Mulieris Dignitatem*, 15.

is not just for relationships that you may need to let go of or set boundaries around; it is also for relationships that you may need to recommit to or make a higher priority.

For example, if you know you are not being faithful to your parents by silencing their calls and making excuses not to visit them, maybe this is because you feel hurt by them in the past, and you are allowing your anger to control your relationship. If you neglect your daily prayer time, maybe this is because you fear if you give God that time, you will not have enough left over to accomplish all of the items on your to do list.

For those relationships in which your fidelity may be emotionally disordered, ask yourself why. What are the underlying issues that either keep you in a possibly unhealthy relationship or prevent you from being further committed to a meaningful relationship? Finally, take these questions to prayer and maybe a trusted friend, priest, or counselor who can help you sort through your thoughts.

Discussion Questions

1. Can you identify with the gift of fidelity? Why or why not?
    What factors in your life have either stifled or encouraged
    growth in this gift?

2. How have you seen women's fidelity make a unique impact
    on your community or in your own life?

3. How does knowing the significance of the women at the Cross
    change how you view the stories of Jesus' passion, death,
    and resurrection?

4. What did you find most inspiring about the women at the Cross?
    What lessons on the feminine genius gift of fidelity can you
    learn from them?

5. Have you ever been in a relationship where you knew you needed
    to make a change, but your emotions prevented you from doing
    so? How did you proceed in the situation?

6. What is one way that you can reveal the gift of fidelity to your
    family, friends, community, or world?

CHAPTER 9

Strength and the Women of the French Revolution

Science shows that men excel at physical strength. In general, men's bones are denser, their muscle mass is larger, their lung capacity is greater, and they are taller than women, on average. These features have proven useful in waging wars and building empires, which tend to be the stuff that history is made of. For this reason, men's strength often dominates history while women's strength receives much less attention. This is because a woman's strength is not like that of a man. Her strength is primarily internal—and when it comes to this hidden, interior strength, life proves that here, women excel.

Interior Strength

God made women strong. Having entrusted humanity to them "always and in every way,"[103] he knew that they *needed* to be strong. It is no small task to care for people, especially in our broken world filled with hardships. When times are tough, according to St. John Paul II, the *"awareness of this entrusting"* is precisely what gives

---

103 John Paul II, *Mulieris Dignitatem*, 30.

women the strength to carry on rather than being overwhelmed with their task of caring for others. In other words, knowing that people are counting on them to be strong makes them strong.

Perhaps you have experienced this interior strength of woman before. In times of crisis—when someone is severely ill, after someone has passed away, during a natural disaster—it is often women who have their eyes on everything. They constantly look around to make sure everyone has what they need and are OK. Even if they are struggling and are on the brink of falling apart, they often find a way to stay strong for others.

This ability is no secret in the Church, and some of my favorite Church writings on women point to this interior feminine strength. In 1947, Venerable Pius XII held up the strength of women in World War II, writing, "The years of World War II and the post-war years have presented … a tragic picture without precedent. Never … have events required on the part of woman so much initiative and daring, so much sense of responsibility, so much fidelity, moral strength, spirit of sacrifice and endurance of all kinds of sufferings—in a word, so much heroism."[104] In 2004, after praising women for their "capacity for the other," Cardinal Ratzinger (the future Benedict XVI) writes, "It is women, in the end, who even in very desperate situations, as attested by history past and present, possess a singular capacity to persevere in adversity, to keep life going even in extreme situations, to hold tenaciously to the future, and finally to remember with tears the value of every human life."[105]

When the world is falling apart, women have the strength to hold together.

Reflecting the thoughts of his brother popes, John Paul II writes

---

104 Pius XII, *Papal Directives for the Woman of Today* (1947), available at papalencyclicals.net/.
105 Ratzinger and Amato, 13.

that "women are owed much by their families, and sometimes by whole nations" for the strength they have imparted for the sake of others.[106] As history repeatedly shows, when faced with seemingly insurmountable challenges, women find strength. Of all the periods in history where this strength manifested itself, few are more evident than the French Revolution.

Meet the Women of the French Revolution

While I find history fascinating, not much of it from grade school through college sunk in. So when my graduate school offered a history course on women of the Church, I immediately signed up. In the class, we explored the lives and experiences of canonized and non-canonized women who lived from the fourteenth to nineteenth centuries. As the semester progressed, I came to realize just how much of history I had missed, and the details of the French Revolution were no exception.

When this topic first came up, I tried to dig back to my limited memories of the event. Guillotines, angry peasants, something about Marie Antoinette telling the poor who had no bread to eat cake, and the end of the French monarchy were about all I could remember. As you can imagine, once the lectures began, I quickly learned that many of the details of the Revolution either never made it into my previous history courses, or I had forgotten them. This reality was especially true when it came to the Revolution's impact on the Catholic Church.

While the Revolution did include the topics I remembered—save the part about eating cake; Marie Antoinette never actually said that—what my history classes did seem to omit from the story is that getting rid of the monarchy was not enough for the revolutionaries. They believed achieving the Revolution's goal of liberty and

---

106 John Paul II, 30.

equality for all would only be possible if the government controlled the Church as well. As time went on, for some, even this was not enough. Some revolutionaries believed they needed to wipe out the Catholic Church in France altogether. As the effects of these beliefs began to take shape, it became clear that to save their country's soul, France needed the feminine genius strength of women now more than ever.

The Catholic Church and the Revolution

Perhaps, like me, your history lessons left out the French Revolution's impact on the Church. Even if not, a few more details on the Church, women, and the Revolution will be helpful before moving on.

At the start of the Revolution in 1789, revolutionaries formed the National Constituent Assembly. This Assembly, which took on various names throughout the Revolution, represented France's middle and lower classes. Because these classes comprised ninety-eight percent of French citizens, they demanded the Assembly be given more weight in decision making. Gaining this right, they immediately began to use their political power to attempt to nationalize the Catholic Church. One of their first moves toward achieving this goal was to require priests to take an oath of fidelity to the new government-run church. Those who refused the oath became known as "nonjuring priests" and were replaced by "juring priests" who pledged their allegiance to the new national church.

With a plan for priests in place, the Assembly knew it would also need to contend with France's many religious communities. To start, revolutionaries orchestrated a governmental takeover of all Church property, including monasteries. Noting that citizens funded the construction of these buildings with their tithes, the Assembly argued that these buildings lawfully belonged to the people of France, not the Church.

Next, similar to Protestant reformers, revolutionary leaders believed that marriage was the only natural state for women. Hoping to empty convents with little push back, government officials met privately with nuns to allow them to declare their desire to leave the convent discretely. However, much to the officials' surprise, most religious sisters refused their offer of "liberation" and expressed their intention to remain in their vocation. Frustrated by their obstinance, the Assembly banned communities from admitting new members and argued that even "useful" communities who performed charitable works would one day become obsolete as the need for charity would lessen without Catholics who enabled the poor with free handouts. In the end, controlling religious orders proved to be a challenge, so in 1792 the Assembly outlawed them entirely and forced all convents to close.

In 1793, revolutionaries guillotined King Louis XVI. Soon after, things went from bad to worse when Maximilian Robespierre gained power and led France into a nearly yearlong period known as the Reign of Terror. During this time, thousands of suspected enemies of the Revolution, many of whom were dissenting priests and religious sisters, were beheaded without a fair trial. Additionally, revolutionary leaders abandoned the idea of a national church in favor of strictly banning the Catholic Faith in any shape or form.

To help move this new direction along, revolutionaries implemented a new, ten-day a week calendar. This change removed both the observance of Sunday Mass and annual feast days, the very staples of Catholic practice. Without Sundays, the only "services" offered were those held by the government-approved "Cult of Reason." Held on the tenth day of the week, these gatherings took place in a "Temple of Reason" and honored the "Supreme Being."

With their nation falling apart, their faith forced underground, and the guillotine an ever-present reality, faithful Catholic Frenchwomen had no choice but to use their interior strength to hold on as they tried to keep things together for their families and communities. Mustering up all the courage they could find, they became living proof of what John Paul II would observe centuries later when he wrote: "The Church sees in the face of women ... the strength that is capable of bearing the greatest sorrows."[107]

The Martyrs of Compiègne

Of the brave women who used their strength to bear "the greatest sorrows" during the French Revolution, perhaps the most well documented are the Carmelite martyrs of Compiègne. Like many religious women during the Protestant Reformation, they too refused to abandon their vocation as a bride of Christ. Despite being turned out of their convent, the sisters defied orders to disband and continued to live as a community.

This decision cost them their lives. Just ten days before the Reign of Terror ended, revolutionaries guillotined all sixteen members of the community for crimes against the Revolution. Like St. Edith Stein, these nuns saw their deaths as a sacrificial offering for the atonement of sins and restoration of peace in their country. In giving of themselves to the point of death, they believed they could help save the spiritual body of Christ, the Church.

I have often wondered if these Carmelites knew the stories of the faithful sisters of the Reformation who went before them and if they found strength in their courage. Likewise, I have also wondered if St. Edith Stein knew the story of these Carmelites who went before *her* and if she found strength in *their* courage. At least for St. Edith Stein, a Carmelite herself, it is almost certain that she would have known about these brave women because, in 1931, German author Gertrud von Le Fort wrote *Song of the Scaffold*, which documents their story.

---

107 John Paul II, *Redemptoris Mater*, 46.

These connections show how much can be learned from women who have gone before us. Yet the martyrs of Compiègne are not the only women of the Revolution who set an example of heroic strength. In fact, their story is not the main story we will consider in this chapter. Instead, for the gift of strength, we will turn to ordinary women who displayed extraordinary strength that defied the course of the Revolution.

Unlikely Adversaries

The center of activity during the French Revolution was Paris. While most decisions, fighting, and beheading happened in and around the capital city, all of France was affected by the Revolution's decrees. Throughout the countryside, news of the Revolution trickled in as peasant women watched and waited for rumored changes to take place in their villages.

These unassuming, humble women spent their days busy with domestic chores to keep their families fed and cared for. They were uneducated and most could not read or write. They held no political power, and, even with the Revolution's claim to bring equality to all, they were not allowed to vote. By and large, they faithfully attended Sunday Mass, said their prayers, and observed liturgical seasons filled with days of fasting and feasting. The names of these women are unknown, yet their stories live on because they became "the woman in Revolution whose specter [haunted] the politicians of the nineteenth century."[108]

Fortress Faith

As the decrees of the Revolution made their way to peasant villages, perhaps one of the first changes faithful Catholics encountered was the installment of a new juring priest. These

108 Olwen H. Hufton, *Women and the Limits of Citizenship in the French Revolution* (Toronto: University of Toronto Press, 2015), 96.

priests, who replaced the local parish priest, were rarely given a warm welcome by the women of their congregations because they had betrayed the Church by taking the oath of fidelity to the government. To these women, the juring priests were intruders. So they boycotted their Masses, skipped their confession lines, did not bring their babies to them to be baptized, and refused to call on them for last rites. Instead, for all of their sacramental needs, faithful women went straight to nonjuring priests secretly harbored by their community.

Widows and spinsters proved to be those most likely to shelter these renegade priests and were often their primary support.[109] As such, they helped organize underground Masses in private homes, barns, or illicit chapels. They passed out anti-oath pamphlets, which condemned the Assembly for forcing priests to pledge allegiance to the national church, and they even protested the oath by organizing petitions.

Since access to a nonjuring priest was not always readily available, mothers worked hard to ensure that some flame of faith was kept alive in their children during the Revolution. As historian Olwen Hufton put it, Catholicism "progressively became a fortress faith"—a faith attacked from without and defended from within— and the task of keeping the faith alive naturally fell to women as "it was driven back into the home."[110] While the circumstances were certainly not ideal, this reality gave mothers more control over their children's experiences with faith.

From their homes' secrecy, mothers did what they could to ensure their Catholic traditions and prayers were taught and practiced. Chief among these was the Rosary, which soared in popularity during the Revolution. Due to its easy-to-memorize prayers, the devotion was practical for the illiterate and required no priest.[111]

---

109 Hufton, 104.
110 Hufton, 108.
111 Hufton, 108.

Knowing full well that each of these actions was a crime against the Revolution, faithful women still chose to take the risk and use their feminine genius strength to persevere for those entrusted to them. However, working independently to preserve the Faith was not the only approach peasant women took to combat the Revolution. As attempts to squelch the Catholic Faith moved deeper into their villages, they quickly realized that there was strength in their numbers.

Strength in Numbers

To nationalize France's religion, the Assembly knew it needed to rid their land of any ties to the Church. From seemingly minor, external signs of worship, such as bell towers, small statutes, and crucifix necklaces, to significant signs, such as church buildings and rectories, it all had to go.[112] As revolutionary officials moved into villages to officiate these removals, groups of peasant women were there to greet them.

To protect the bell tower that chimed for prayer, the women of Avallon camped out in the tower to prevent its destruction. Holding up a crucifix from their perch, they yelled at their adversaries, "Here, see our master who chases you!"[113] Or when the Assembly sold the church rectory in Sacy, the women protested to their local official stating the building belonged to them. When their pleas fell on deaf ears, the women proceeded to remove and hide all of the building's doors and windows, not once, but twice.[114]

For these women, these buildings were not just buildings; they were icons of their communities' faith and belonged to their communities

---

112 Hufton, 115.

113 Suzanne Desan, "The Role of Women in Religious Riots During the French Revolution," *Eighteenth-Century Studies* 22, no. 3 (Spring 1989): 455, https://doi.org/10.2307/2738896.

114 Desan, 456.

because they were built by the labor and funding of their ancestors.[115] Protecting them was protecting what God entrusted to them through the hands of those who had gone before them.

Physical symbols of the Catholic Church were not the only threat to the Assembly's goal of creating an independent, national church. In addition to removing the Catholic cultural symbols, the Revolution also needed to reeducate its population with new doctrines. Forcing priests to sign oaths of fidelity and banning religious orders were a start, but these actions did not stop lay educators from teaching the Faith. Chief among these educators were women known as "béates."

Béates were widows or spinsters who lived in village-owned homes in exchange for educating young girls.[116] These women organized work sessions in which they would teach a local trade *and* the catechism. Additionally, in winter months, when traveling to the village church was impossible, they organized Sunday services which included reading from Scripture and singing hymns. Béates were a staple of French Catholicism and, therefore, a threat to the Revolution.

In the summer of 1793, just months before the start of the Reign of Terror, the Assembly placed a man named Solon Reynaud over the French department of Haute-Loire.[117] An ex-priest turned government official, Solon was eager to prove himself and came into the area with an iron fist. Besides setting up a local guillotine and strictly enforcing new national practices, such as civil marriage and non-sacramental burial ceremonies, Solon decided to go after the béates.

In an attempt to control them, Solon sent one of his subordinates to the village of Montpigié and charged him with conducting a béate oath of fidelity ceremony. The official invited all of the women in the

---

115 Desan, 456.
116 Hufton, 114.
117 In 1790, the National Constituent Assembly rid the nation of its provinces and divided France into eighty-three "departments."

area to witness this event. Underestimating the women's numbers and their fidelity to the Church, the ceremony was a disaster. When the béates declared they preferred the guillotine over loyalty to a pagan regime, about a hundred women stood by their sides, and together they were all taken to the local prison. However, just hours later, the husbands of the incarcerated rebels found themselves struggling with household chores and children. Unhappy with the situation, they demanded the release of their wives.[118] Within a few days, officials released everyone but the béates. Determined to liberate their comrades, the women regrouped, took the prison by storm, freed the béates, and locked up Solon's representative.

Revealing the Gift of Strength

When the French Revolution began, revolutionaries never dreamed that rural peasant women would cause them so much trouble. In fact, many assumed that peasant men would happily embrace the Revolution and their "irrational" and "slow-witted" wives would blindly follow.[119] As time would prove, they could not have been more wrong.

Unable to even vote, peasant women of the Revolution rarely tried to change laws or influence political leaders because that was nearly impossible. However, they did whatever they could to preserve the Catholic Faith in their own homes and communities. During some of the most challenging times of the Revolution, these women used their interior feminine strength to hold on and persevere for those they loved. Most of their actions seemed small—saving a bell tower, sheltering a priest, hosting an underground Mass, teaching the Rosary to their children, standing up for a béate—yet when they mixed each of these small actions with the grace of God, *the* Catholic soul of France was able to endure.

---

118 Hufton, 117.
119 Hufton, 99.

By 1795, the Reign of Terror was in the past, and Catholic worship was once again permitted, albeit with strict parameters. However, plans for controlled worship were doomed to fail because the difficult years of the Revolution did not destroy the faith of steadfast Catholics; rather, it strengthened it. A new revival of the Faith was underway, and, in every region, women were leading the charge.[120]

This female-led revival fashioned a century filled with unbelievable graces for France. All of the Rosaries prayed while the Church was underground led to a surge in Marian devotion. A few decades later, Mary would appear to St. Bernadette as Our Lady of Lourdes and to St. Margaret Mary Alacoque as Our Lady of Grace. Additionally, some of France's greatest saints were shaped by this century—saints such as St. Thérèse of Lisieux and St. John Vianney. In fact, St. John Vianney grew up during the Revolution attending underground Mass with his family, and he received catechism instruction in secret by two sheltered nuns.

None of this would have been possible without the relentless strength of the peasant women who went before them. If not for religious women, like the Martyrs of Compiègne, who used their strength to offer themselves for the Church, or for the brave peasant women, who used their strength to hold on for those entrusted to them, France may have lost its Catholic identity forever. These women proved that physical strength used in wars and revolutions is no match for the interior strength of a woman who fights for the people entrusted to her, "always and in every way."[121]

How Can Strength Get Twisted?

The feminine genius is person-oriented. Therefore, it finds its strength in being strong for others. Even when it seems that a woman needs

---

120 Hufton, 122.
121 John Paul II, *Mulieris Dignitatem*, 30.

to be strong for nobody's sake but her own, she is actually fighting for others as she fights for herself. For example, a mother might continue to fight a physical or mental illness because she can be more present to her children with progressive healing. An employee might persevere in a stressful work situation because she cares about those she serves. Or a friend might fight to work through past trauma so in the future she can help others with their journey of recovery. While these are situations that require personal interior strength, their end goal is still focused on others.

Sometimes, however, we can easily lose sight of this motivation for others and allow our strength to become entirely self-focused. It is understandable why this can happen. We live in a broken world, and as a result, people can make a mess out of life. They say and do hurtful things that lead to disappointment, pain, and scars. When this happens, it can be easy to build walls around our hearts and cut ourselves off from life and love. For women, this is a dangerous place to be because *they have the interior strength to do it*. They have what it takes to push people out and hold onto grudges. They have what it takes to settle into bitterness. Instead of using their strength to bring people together, they can use it to keep people away.

What Can We Do About It?

If you have ever used your interior strength to hold onto a grudge or harden your heart, you know that the person you end up hurting the most is yourself. God created us for relationships. He made us to love and be loved. If someone is not free to do this, then he or she needs healing—and one of the first steps in the healing process is learning to use one's interior strength to let go.

This is easier said than done, of course. It requires trust, vulnerability, and forgiveness—none of which is easy. The good news, though, is that none of us is expected to do it alone. Like with every feminine genius gift, the ability to live from strength is ultimately not mustered up from one's own power; rather, it is accomplished through the grace of God. Ultimately, *he* is the one who gives us the strength to let go. The key is inviting him into our brokenness and allowing him to do his work.

Strength Challenge

It is time to get practical. The implication that you should "just let God give you his grace to help you" is not very helpful. If you are using your interior strength to hold on in a way that hurts you in the long run, I want to share with you a challenge that my spiritual director, Sister Susan, has given to me.

To help let go of a grudge, wall, burden, or situation that you want to be free of, I invite you to write a letter to Jesus. In the letter, explain everything about the situation that is stealing your peace. It does not have to be well-written or even coherent; just put all of your thoughts and feeling on paper. Then, bring it with you the next time you go to Mass, in your pocket or purse. At the procession of the gifts, imagine your letter being carried up the aisle with the bread and wine. As it reaches the altar, in your heart, surrender the contents of the letter to our Lord. "Here it is, Jesus. Everything you need to know about ____. All my thoughts, all my feelings—I give them to you. Unite them with your suffering and give me the grace to let go."

This simple act has done a lot for me when I needed to surrender life's challenges to the Lord. I have noticed, though, that as soon as I give something to him, I try to take it back. If you are like me, you will need to do what I often do—bring the letter back again the next time you go to Mass. And the next time ... and the time after that ... until one day you forget to bring the letter with you. When this happens, you will know that you genuinely are starting to let go.

Discussion Questions

1. Can you identify with the gift of strength? Why or why not? What factors in your life have either stifled or encouraged growth in this gift?

2. When in your life have you experienced the interior strength of women during a crisis?

3. If you lived during the French Revolution, how do you think you would have responded to the Assembly's attempts to remove the Catholic Faith from France? Are there any similarities between our world today and the world of the Revolution a few centuries ago?

4. What did you find most inspiring about the women of the French Revolution? What lessons on the feminine genius gift of strength can you learn from them?

5. Is there a time in your life where you knew your strength came from the Lord? What were the circumstances of the situation?

6. What is one way that you can reveal the gift of strength to your family, friends, community, or world?

CHAPTER 10

The Ideal Woman

After eight gifts, examples, explorations, and challenges, St. John Paul II's request for us to "reflect carefully on what it means to speak of the *'genius of women,'*"[122] is nearly complete. Yet one thing remains. Now we need to bring it all together by considering the question, "What does authentic femininity look like today?" To begin, let's take an "ideal woman" trip down memory lane.

Fifty Years, Three Ideals

The iconic image of a housewife from the 1950s is one you are likely familiar with. In her tea-length dress with pearls and heels, she cooked, cleaned, and ironed with a smile. She was a domestic goddess, who was not only cute as a button but knew how to sew one too. In the '50s and early '60s, being the flawless queen of the castle was the ideal every woman strove for, but this path to feminine perfection did not continue forever.

By the end of the 1960s, the sexual revolution had taken ahold of American culture, and with it came the rise of hippies and radical male-bashing feminists. In this era, the ideal woman was

---

122 John Paul II, *Letter to Women*, 10.

encouraged to let go of her inhibitions and go with the flow. She was taught that traditional gender roles were holding her back and a male hierarchy was oppressing her. Not wanting to be limited to domestic chores and childrearing, she rejected her mother's domestic goddess role and paved a new trail that liberated her from motherhood altogether.

By the 1980s, however, many free-loving feminists began to recognize that men were taking advantage of them. Deep down, feminine intuition told these women that they were not made to be treated as sexual objects for another's physical pleasure. However, rather than listen to this intuition, many determined that the new answer was to let go of their feminine tendencies and assert themselves like men. Men seemed better at emotionally detaching themselves from others, which made actions like no-strings-attached sex easier. As the logic went, if men could do it, women could do it too.

When you put it all together, in just over fifty years, the world gave women three very different directives for what the ideal woman should look and act like. In the '50s and early '60s, she was a domestic goddess. In the late '60s and '70s, she was a free-loving feminist. In the '80s and '90s, she was a woman asserting herself like a man. In reflecting on these rapid changes, I found myself wondering how I would have measured up in each of the different eras.

Measuring Up

To start, the domestic goddess ideal of the '50s and early '60s is one that I would have surely failed at. When it comes to cooking, nobody has ever called me "a natural." In my first few years of marriage, I floundered around my tiny galley kitchen, baking flat cookies, burning instant rice, and trying to turn raw chicken white by boiling it. Once kids came on the scene, I was so overwhelmed by the constant mess that I hired college students to help me clean our tiny apartment. And ironing? My definition of ironing has and always will be a spray bottle filled with water. So no, if I had been an adult woman in the 1950s and early '60s, *Good Housekeeping* would never have come knocking on my door for a feature entitled "How I Do It All."

How about the late '60s and '70s? How would I have fared in the era of the hippie feminist? Not well. First, I am "Type A"—or as my husband likes to say, "Type A+." I like order and predictability, which means that the idea of "going with the flow" puts me on edge. Next, I like my inhibitions because they stop me from doing stupid things. Finally, I do not hate men; I actually really like them, especially the one I married. So once again, had I been an adult woman during this era, *Rolling Stone* would have looked the other way in its search for an ideal woman of the time to feature.

While I would have fallen on my face as an ideal woman in those first two eras, when it comes to the '80s, I think I could have partially swung it as a cultural example of womanhood. The whole "Women, let's take over the world!" gig kind of sounds fun to me because I like being in charge. Remember those group projects we all did in grade school? For me, those were not "group projects," those were "Lisa projects," and my job was to convince everyone else that their menial role was vital while I did all the actual work. Why? Well, if someone was not doing things my way, they were not doing things the *right way*.

Thankfully, through my great formation later in life, I learned that authentic leadership is not about clawing your way to the top. Instead, it is about serving those you are leading. Therefore, despite secular wisdom that pushed women to become the "boss witch," I never actually jumped on the bandwagon. Anyway, there is also the issue of shoulder pads. That is one fashion move I just cannot pull off, so you would never see me donning them on the cover of *Ms.* magazine.

Cultural Trends

As history has proven, society has a lot to say regarding what the ideal woman should look like. Unfortunately, as many women have found, trying to live up to these ever-changing standards of womanhood can be exhausting. Yet so many women still try to reach for the world's ideal, which is exactly what the secular culture wants. Why? Because the world knows that if it can control who a woman thinks she *should* be, then it can control a woman.

For a woman who is chasing after an ideal set by the world, where she shops, how she recreates, what media she consumes, the types of foods she eats—whether she realizes it or not—each of these decisions is influenced by what the world tells her a woman should like, do, and be. Her thoughts on morality, religion, and politics become formed by a voice that whispers an ever-evolving version of truth. When this voice is listened to, it shapes what she believes about sex, marriage, and motherhood—all of which are foundational to society.

Maybe you already know this, and you do not take your cues from our culture. But maybe it is not secular culture that leaves you feeling pressured to live up to a standard. Maybe it is the culture within your church community.

Even within our Catholic communities, it can be easy to want to measure up to an ever-shifting set of criteria for what a Catholic woman *should* look like. While a Catholic community is a wonderful support and can be a great place to turn to for examples of women seeking to live authentic femininity, it is important to separate what is essential versus non-essential in femininity.

Maybe your wardrobe, job, or hobbies are perfectly moral, but they still do not fit your community's mold. Maybe you feel inadequate because you are not good at stereotypical feminine activities that are praised in your parish. Maybe you do not know what stance you are "supposed" to take on non-essential trending issues, or what Catholic social media accounts you "should" follow, or even what Catholic planner you "need" to own. Any of these perceived deficiencies can leave you feeling "less than" as a Catholic woman, so it is important to be careful not to let Catholic trends create confusion about what constitutes authentic femininity.

Finding Examples

Finding an example of a culture that perfectly lived femininity is impossible. Even if I wanted to point out an exemplary time and place for all women to imitate, I could not because it doesn't exist. Sure, some cultures have done better than others, but there is not one period or community to point to and say, "Here. These women fully understood, valued, and lived from their femininity." Yet, in every time and place, certain women revealed their genius in brilliant ways.

Many of these brilliant women have been our guides throughout this book. From married to single to religious to consecrated lay women; from those with doctorates in philosophy to those who were unable to read; from rich to poor; from long lives to short ones—each of these women revealed their genius in their unique circumstances. Their diversity shows us that authentic femininity does not fit into one tiny box; rather, within the feminine genius there is so much room for each individual to live and breathe from the unique expressions of their gifts. Additionally, the criteria for their femininity did not depend upon their sense of fashion, ability to cook, job title, or knowledge of the latest Catholic trends. It came down to the ways they loved the Lord and those he entrusted to them, even in their human imperfections.

In seeking to live as authentic Catholic women, sometimes they made mistakes, lived selfishly, or failed to be strong for others.

But they never gave up, and their lives can, and should, inspire us. However, none of them ever became the ideal woman that every other woman should imitate. In fact, becoming the ideal woman was just as impossible for them as it is for us because none of us is perfect.

Throughout all of history, there is only one woman who was perfect. This woman lived her feminine genius in a way that each of us can strive to imitate. She is the only ideal woman to ever walk this earth. While we, who are imperfect, cannot become ideal women, we can strive to become *authentic* women by following her example, just as the women we have seen in this book did.

Who is the ideal woman? She is Jesus' mother and ours—Mary. If you ever want to know what it means to be a woman, you can always turn to her.

Mary—The Ideal Woman

The fact that Mary was perfect, and thus the ideal woman, can make it hard to connect with her. After all, she was sinless, and we are ... not. Knowing this can make her example feel a bit invalid, as if authentic womanhood is only possible for someone who is sinless. But although Mary was the ideal woman who always said yes to God, it is essential to remember that she was still fully human. Just like the rest of us, she had free will. God did not force her to be the mother of Jesus; she chose to say "yes."

Additionally, although Mary was sinless, she was not free from human limitations, such as hunger and exhaustion, nor did she lack human emotions. For example, when the angel Gabriel greeted her at the Annunciation, she was "greatly troubled" (Luke 1:29); or when the child Jesus went missing on the way home from Jerusalem, she "anxiously" looked for him (Luke 2:48). These feelings, along with a host of others, were felt in the depths of Mary's being as she processed all the events happening around her, "pondering them in her heart" (Luke 2:19).

By looking beneath the surface-level impressions one might get from a pious statue or pristine painting of Mary, it becomes easier to see an image of her humanity—a humanity that felt deeply and loved intensely, a humanity that used every fiber of her feminine genius to care for those entrusted to her, a humanity that, according to St. John Paul II, makes Mary *"the highest expression of the 'feminine genius.'"* [123]

Every single feminine genius gift we have explored here can be found in the life of Mary. She exuded the feminine genius. While none of us can reach her perfection, her life gives us a perfect example as we strive to live authentically as women.

Mary's Self-Giving and Generosity

Mary exuded feminine *self-giving* and *generosity.* Her entire life was a complete gift of self to God the Father, his Son Jesus, and the whole world. From the first moment Mary came on the scene in the Gospels, at the Annunciation, she was committed to giving generously of herself.

Along with the news of her miraculous pregnancy, Gabriel also told Mary of the miraculous pregnancy of her elderly cousin Elizabeth. With her own pregnancy, Mary's to-do list instantly became quite long, but she put aside all thoughts of herself and ran "with haste" to be with Elizabeth (Luke 1:39). Upon arrival, she generously stayed to accompany her cousin for three months.

Whatever plans Mary may have had for her future, the moment the angel Gabriel showed up, they immediately changed. She said yes, and from that moment, she generously gave her entire being to the Lord in a new and profound way.

Having carried four babies of my own, I can say that Mary's visit to Elizabeth was no small act of self-giving generosity. Mary was

---

123 John Paul II, 10.

in the *first trimester* of her pregnancy when she traveled to see her cousin. If ever there is a time when I want to do nothing but lay on a couch and let people attend to me, it is during the first trimester of pregnancy. Any woman who has experienced it will tell you that those three months are exhausting. Yet here is Mary, giving, loving, and serving as the handmaid of the Lord.

Handmaid? Yes. As St. John Paul II writes, "Mary called herself the 'handmaid of the Lord.' ... Putting herself at God's service, she also put herself at the service of others."[124] When you hear "handmaid," the first thing you have to do is get some modern notions of the word out of your mind. No one forced Mary into subjecting herself. She freely chose to give herself in service to a loving God and his people.

If you ever feel like you have nothing to give, turn to Mary. She knows human fatigue, and she also knows how to find much-needed rest in the Lord.

Mary's Receptivity

Mary exuded feminine *receptivity*, which one can easily see in her "yes" to receiving Jesus into her body through the power of the Holy Spirit. Through that *fiat*, her entire life became a yes to the will of God because being the Mother of God is not a short-term commitment. Rather than being overwhelmed by this life-altering role, she actively received it.

When Mary arrived at Elizabeth's house, she had a story to tell. If I were Mary, after greeting Elizabeth, I would probably have declared that the whole thing was insane and then gone off on a monologue about how I felt. *An angel showed up asking if I would become the mother of God! Elizabeth, I don't know what I was thinking, but I said yes. Now, what am I supposed to do? Pregnant*

---

124 John Paul II, 10.

before my marriage is finalized? This is the kind of stuff people get stoned for!

This would have been my approach, but it was not Mary's. She actively received the gift and responded with a song of praise. As Mary proclaims in the Magnificat, "My soul magnifies the Lord, and my spirit rejoices in God my Savior, for he has regarded the low estate of his handmaiden. For behold, henceforth all generations will call me blessed; for he who is mighty has done great things in me, and holy is his name" (Luke 1:46-49).

When we are struggling to receive whatever the Lord desires to give us, both trials and blessings, turning to Mary for inspiration can provide us with strength. As John Paul II writes, "In Mary all are called to put total trust in the divine omnipotence, which transforms hearts, guiding them toward full receptivity to his providential plan of love."[125]

Mary's Maternity

Mary exuded feminine *maternity* as she worked to "cherish, guard, protect, nourish and advance [the] growth" of Jesus.[126]

It might be easy to think that being the Mother of God would make maternity easy, but remember: Mary gave birth in a *stable*. Despite the unconventional setting, she found ways to nurture her newborn baby. Wrapping Jesus up tight into swaddling clothes, or as we like to call it in our house, a baby burrito, she knew the tricks that moms still use today. Resourceful like all moms, without a bed for her precious child, she made a soft place for him to lay in the manger. In those early days, she even managed to open up her temporary home to visitors such as shepherds and wise men.

---

125 John Paul II, General Audience (November 29, 1995), in *John Paul II Speaks on Women*, para. 5.

126 Stein, *Essays on Woman*, 45.

During those precious hidden years while Jesus grew up, Mary was surely attentive to his needs as, like all mothers, she delighted in his milestones. His first smile, the first time he rolled over, his first words and steps—each of these must have made her heart soar as her little boy grew up to be a man.

Mary is not just Jesus' mother; she is our mother, too. From her place in heaven as Queen Mother, Mary selflessly labors to "cherish, guard, protect, nourish and advance [our] growth" as she spiritually mothers us.[127] As John Paul II writes, "The maternal 'reign' of Mary consists in this, she who was, in all her being, a gift for her Son, *has also become a gift for the sons and daughters of the whole human race,* awakening profound trust in those who seek her guidance along the difficult paths of life."[128] Like any good mother, Mary never turns away those who ask for her help. Offering her prayers and support, Mary's guidance and love always lead us toward her Son and show us what it truly means to be maternal.

Mary's Sensitivity and Intuition

Mary exuded feminine *sensitivity* and *intuition*. Understanding the human heart, she saw and found ways to meet the needs of those around her.

As the precious hidden years of Jesus' life came to a close, the Gospel of John reveals that Mary was still by thirty-year-old Jesus' side as they attended an out-of-town wedding together in Cana (see John 2:1-12). During the festivities, Mary noticed that the newlywed couple was running out of wine. Such an occurrence would have been as embarrassing as forgetting silverware for a dinner party. Yet Mary knew what to do. She brought the need to

---

127 Stein, 45.

128 John Paul II, *Letter to Women*, 10.

her Son Jesus. Trusting that he would take care of it for her, she left the request in his hands, and before long, Jesus miraculously turned six stone jars of water into wine. John Paul II recounts the significance of this episode:

> At Cana in Galilee there is shown only one concrete aspect of human need, apparently a small one of little importance ("They have no wine"). But it has a symbolic value ... Mary places herself between her Son and mankind in the reality of their wants, needs, and sufferings ... not as an outsider, but in her position as mother. She knows that as such she can point out to her Son the needs of mankind.[129]

Mary knows our hearts because her Immaculate Heart is sensitive to her spiritual sons and daughters. She intuitively knows what each of us needs and presents these needs to Jesus because, like any good son, he listens to her. In attuning our hearts to the Immaculate Heart of Mary, we too can learn how to see the needs of others and care for them with sensitivity and intuition like Mary.[130]

Mary's Fidelity

Mary exuded feminine *fidelity*. Before anyone else followed Jesus, Mary was there. She was his first disciple, the first to believe in him, and the first to learn from him. More than any other person in his life, she knew him, and she was limitlessly faithful to him as she followed him wherever his life took her.

After the challenge of giving birth in a stable, Mary quickly learned that her adventures as the Mother of God had only just begun. When the wise men packed up and headed back east, an angel came to Joseph in a dream and warned him not to take Jesus back to Nazareth. King Herod wanted Jesus dead, and the only way to

---

129 John Paul II, *Redemptoris Mater*, 21.

130 Alexandra Richards Cathey, "Unlocking the Feminine Genius with Edith Stein" (Master's thesis, Holy Apostles College and Seminary, 2017), 94.

protect the newborn King was to flee to Egypt (see Matthew 2:13). To protect her Son, Mary left the support of her family and friends and lived her early years of motherhood as a refugee in a foreign country, with its own unique culture, language, and food. At times, this must have been challenging and lonely, but she faithfully did whatever it took to care for her Son.

"Mary followed Jesus step by step in her maternal pilgrimage of faith," St. John Paul II writes. "She followed him during the years of his hidden life at Nazareth; she followed him also during the time after he left home, when he began 'to do and to teach' in the midst of Israel. Above all she followed him in the tragic experience of Golgotha ... yet not even beneath the Cross did Mary's faith fail."[131] Through it all, Mary can show us what it means to be there for others and to trust in her Son with complete fidelity.

Mary's Strength

Finally, Mary exuded feminine *strength*. Upon saying yes to becoming the Mother of God, Mary could not have known exactly what her yes would hold. However, when she presented her infant son at the Temple, the prophet Simeon gave her a glimpse. He foretold to her that her Son was destined to be "the fall and rising of many in Israel" and, in the process, "a sword will also pierce through your own soul" (Luke 2:35).

Can you imagine knowing that your precious child of just forty days would one day be a source of suffering for you? Then, you spend your life not knowing exactly when this suffering would come to fruition? It must have taken an immense amount of strength to bear this knowledge and still be present at each moment. Yet Mary chose to stay strong—for her Son and for his followers. And when the time of suffering began, she did not falter. As one of the women

---

131 John Paul II, *Redemptoris Mater*, 26.

at the foot of the Cross, John Paul II was speaking of her when he writes, "As we see, in this most arduous test of faith and fidelity the women proved stronger than the Apostles. In this moment of danger, those who love much succeed in overcoming their fear." [132]

Mary must have been an immense support to the disciples during the Passion of Jesus and the long hours of waiting that followed. Using her feminine strength, combined with an unfailing trust that her Son knew what he was doing, she surely was a ray of hope during a very dark period. When you do not feel strong, turn to Mary. She spent a lifetime using her feminine strength to remain hopeful and be strong for others, and she can show you how to do it too.

Authentic Femininity

Mary is the ideal woman. Of all of the women who have ever existed, she lived her femininity better than them all. If you want to know what it means to be a woman, turn to her in everything. Her example is timeless and transcends any cultural trends because it is not dependent upon the views of a particular time or place; rather, it is rooted in the unchanging and the eternal.

God created every woman, from Eve to the baby girl who was born as you read this sentence, with the same unchanging, ever-relevant foundation. Her value and dignity are not dependent upon her ability to live up to current standards. God made her in his image and likeness, and he is the same yesterday, today, and forever.[133] From the beginning of time, God entrusted her with humanity "always and in every way." [134] To aid her in this entrusting, he has provided her with feminine genius gifts that give her everything she needs to live up to this call, if, like Mary,

---

132 John Paul II, *Mulieris Dignitatem*, 15.

133 John Paul II, 30.

134 John Paul II, 30.

she turns to him for his grace.

If you have ever felt like you are not feminine enough, erase that lie from your memory right now. Maybe you do not fit the mold of our current culture. No problem. In this book, though, did you find ways you have expressed the feminine genius gifts that were presented? Even if you do not live all of these gifts perfectly (none of us do!), did you at least see the good in them and *desire* to grow in them in your unique way? If so, then be confident because God is not expecting you to become the *ideal* woman—Mary already has that covered—but he has given you everything you need to become an *authentic* woman. So, what does this authentic woman look like?

She is **self-giving**. Reflecting the love of the Trinity, she too selflessly pours out her love for those entrusted to her.

She is **receptive**. Physically receiving others into her body and invisibly receiving others into her heart, she physically and spiritually brings life into the world.

She is **maternal**. Caring for those entrusted to her, she advances the growth of others as a physical or spiritual mother.

She is **sensitive**. Recognizing both exterior physical needs and deeper interior needs, she sees people with her heart and acknowledges their inherent value.

She is **intuitive**. Knowing what needs to be done and how to do it, she instinctively approaches situations in ways that protect and nourish those entrusted to her.

She is **generous**. Selflessly giving of herself, she does not count the cost as she heroically gives in seemingly ordinary ways.

She is **faithful**. Refusing to give up on those she loves, she is limitlessly faithful to both her God and her people.

She is *strong*. Interiorly holding on when it is easy to give up, she finds the strength to remain resilient for the sake of others.

She is a *woman*. Living from her genius, she makes the world more human.

Vitally Essential

Women are amazing. Imagine how different our world would be if they failed to recognize and live from their feminine genius gifts. Imagine how our broken world would survive without the feminine genius. It could not. In fact, at the closing of the Second Vatican Council, St. Paul VI warned that if women do not live from their feminine gifts, our world runs the risk of becoming "inhumane": "Watch carefully over the future of our [human] race, hold back the hand of man who, in a moment of folly, might attempt to destroy human civilization ... you to whom life is entrusted at this grave moment in history, it is for you to save the peace of the world."[135]

This is why St. John Paul II called the feminine genius "vitally essential."[136] The world needs us. It needs who we are. It needs our self-giving, receptive, maternal, sensitive, intuitive, generous, faithful, and strong person-oriented feminine genius. No matter what this ever-changing world tells you, you have what it takes to be an authentic woman. With Mary as your model and the Lord as your help, do not hold back. Reveal the gift.

---

135 Second Vatican Council, *Address of Pope Paul VI to Women* (December 8, 1965), vatican.va.

136 John Paul II, "Angelus" (July 23, 1995), in *John Paul II Speaks on Women*, para. 2.

Discussion Questions

1. If you were an adult woman in the 1950s through the 1990s, how did you fair compared to the "ideal woman" of the various eras? If you were not an adult during those eras, how do you think you would have fared?

2. In what ways does the world's current definition of femininity affect the way you see yourself and others? Has the culture of a Catholic community ever affected the way you view femininity? If so, how?

3. What do you find most inspiring about the life of Mary? What lessons on any of the feminine genius gifts can you learn from her?

4. After exploring each of the feminine genius gifts presented in this book, which gift do you identify with the most now? Is it a different gift than the one you chose at the beginning of the book, and if so, what do you think accounts for the change?

5. What has been your greatest takeaway from reading this book?

Conclusion

As you finish reading this book, I pray that this is not an end but a beginning for you—a beginning of understanding the gift of your femininity with a whole new light. A start of living from your genius in a whole new way.

Keep the Flame Burning

As I said in the Introduction, even after all of my studying, praying, and reading, I still do not have femininity totally figured out—and I know that this book alone is not enough for you to wholly figure it out, either. But that is OK. This discovery is a lifelong journey, and there is something beautiful about that. The goal is not to make you masters of womanhood but to awaken in you a desire to want to understand and live your feminine genius better. My hope is that a flame has been ignited in your heart to continue to seek out this whole "girl thing." So here are a few action items that you can consider to keep this flame burning.

Cling to women saints. Allow yourself to move past the prejudices that a bonnet-wearing St. Elizabeth Ann Seton or a philosophizing St. Edith Stein can conjure up. The saints are not distant women of the past you cannot relate to. They are your sisters who have gone before you and can show you the way. Read the extended version of their stories and get to know their hearts. Discover who they loved and what they fought for. Seek to understand their struggles and battles. Be inspired by how they became saints. If you commit time to their lives, it will change yours. (Check out the "For Further Reading" list in the appendix to learn more about the women saints we have discussed.)

Cultivate your genius. While the feminine genius is written on our souls and revealed through our bodies, that does not mean that living from it is *perfectly* natural. You can liken many of these gifts to virtues, which means that if you intentionally practice them, you can grow in them. For example, if you want to increase your fidelity, let your "yes mean yes" and make a personal commitment not to cancel on someone unless there is an emergency. If you want to grow in maternity, look for ways to nurture others through volunteering with children, the elderly, or those with special needs. If you desire to cultivate receptivity, host others in your home for dinner or a small group study. (For more ideas, check out "For Further Growth" in the appendix.)

Discover more gifts. I presented to you what I believe are eight foundational gifts of the feminine genius, but as I said at the beginning, they are not the exclusive gifts of the feminine genius. St. John Paul II used other words, such as beauty[137] or humility,[138] when highlighting what women uniquely bring to the world. Reading his writings and those of St. Edith Stein can help you discover more ways that women are amazing.

Pray always. If there is one thing that goes in my obituary when I die, I hope it is, "She was always telling people to pray." Without prayer, there is nothing. If you genuinely want to grow in your understanding of womanhood, prayer is critical. It is in prayer that Jesus can speak to your heart and transform your life. Ask

---

137 See John Paul II, *Letter to Women,* 12; or *Redemptoris Mater,* 26; or General Audience (November 29, 1995), para. 5.

138 See John Paul II, *Mulieris Dignitatem,* 15; or *On the Collaboration of Men and Women in the Church and in the World,* 16.

him to reveal to you the beauty and dignity of your femininity; he will always be your greatest teacher.

Reveal the Gift

Now is the time. Instead of holding back your gifts from the world, take St. Paul VI's closing remarks to the Second Vatican Council to heart:

> The hour is coming, in fact has come, when the vocation of woman is being achieved in its fullness, the hour in which woman acquires in the world an influence, an effect and a power never hitherto achieved. That is why, at this moment when the human race is under-going so deep a transformation, women impregnated with the spirit of the Gospel can do so much to aid mankind in not falling.[139]

Reveal the gift that you are to the world.

I am so grateful that you have finished this book. It is a privilege to share my thoughts and heart with you. My prayers are with you, I promise. And I look forward to seeing how your feminine genius is going to change the world.

---

139 Second Vatican Council, *Address of Pope Paul VI to Women.*

Epilogue

This History of the Feminine Genius

In the late 1980s and early '90s, a marked emphasis on women emerged in St. John Paul II's writings. On New Year's Day of 1987, he proclaimed an international Marian Year, beginning on Pentecost, June 7, 1987 and ending on August 15, 1988, the Solemnity of the Assumption. In anticipation, on March 25, 1987, the Solemnity of the Annunciation, he issued his encyclical *Redemptoris Mater* ("Mother of the Redeemer"). Then, to close out the Marian Year, he issued the apostolic letter *Mulieris Dignitatem* ("On the Dignity and Vocation of Women"), his most in-depth teaching on the meaning of femininity and the role of women in the family, Church, and world.

A few years later, on New Year's Day 1995, John Paul II dedicated his annual World Day of Peace message to the theme "Women: Teachers of Peace." From there, an unofficial "Year of the Woman" arose as he spoke monthly on the topic of women. A highlight of this year was his *Letter of Pope John Paul the Second to Women*, more commonly known as his *Letter to Women*, written for the United Nation's Fourth World Conference on Women held in Beijing, China, in September 1995. The conference's theme was "Equality, Development, and Peace," all of which were reiterated and reflected upon in his pastoral letter.

Threaded throughout each of these documents was the unique, person-oriented contribution that women bring to the world by virtue of their feminine nature. While writing on this gift of womanhood, John Paul II eventually began to refer to it as the "genius of woman" or the "feminine genius."

While John Paul II made these terms famous, he was not the first to use them. To my knowledge, the precise origin of them is unknown. As far back as 1934, however, we can find them used. In her book *The Eternal Woman*, Catholic writer Gertrud von Le Fort briefly speaks on the "genius that is essentially feminine" and "the work of feminine genius." [140] Originally published in German, the work was translated into English in 1954 and is still in print today.

During the same era, another German writer, St. Edith Stein, frequently wrote on feminine genius concepts. However, it does not appear that she used the term "feminine genius" in her writings. Her influence on St. John Paul II's understanding of woman is evident, though, when we compare their words. She undoubtedly inspired John Paul II, who would eventually canonize her and name her one of the six co-patrons of Europe.

Of course, prior to St. John Paul II, the Church was not silent on women in the modern era. Venerable Pius XII writes of the unique gifts and contributions of women in his 1947 letter for the International Union of Catholic Women's Leagues. In 1963, St. John XXIII highlights the increasing influence of women in his encyclical *Pacem in Terris* ("Peace on Earth"). For the closing of the Second Vatican Council in 1965, St. Paul VI wrote a special statement calling women to bring their desperately needed femininity into the world. These are but a few examples of the many times popes have addressed the genius of woman without calling it such.

---

140 Gertrud von Le Fort, *The Eternal Woman* (San Francisco: Ignatius Press, 2010), 33.

Appendix

For Further Reading

On the Feminine Genius

- *Mulieris Dignitatem*, St. John Paul II
- *Letter to Women*, St. John Paul II
- *Redemptoris Mater*, St. John Paul II
- *Pope John Paul II Speaks on Women*, edited by Brooke Williams Deely
- *On the Collaboration of Men and Women in the Church and in the World*, Joseph Cardinal Ratzinger
- *Essays on Woman*, Edith Stein
- *The Privilege of Being a Woman*, Alice von Hildebrand
- *The Eternal Woman*, Gertrud von Le Fort

St. Edith Stein

- *Edith Stein: A Biography*, Waltraud Herbstrith

Servant of God Chiara Corbella Petrillo

- *Chiara Corbella Petrillo: A Witness to Hope*, Simone Troisi and Cristiana Paccini
- See also: chiaracorbellapetrillo.org/en/

St. Elizabeth Ann Seton

- *Elizabeth Seton: American Saint,* Catherine O'Donnell

Servant of God Dorothy Day

- *The Long Loneliness: The Autobiography of the Legendary Catholic Social Activist,* Dorothy Day
- *Dorothy Day: An Introduction to Her Life and Thought,* Terrence C. Wright

St. Catherine of Siena

- *The Life of St. Catherine of Siena: The Classic on Her Life and Accomplishments as Recorded by Her Spiritual Director,* Blessed Raymond of Capua
- *Lay Siege to Heaven: A Novel About St. Catherine of Siena,* Louis de Wohl
- *The Dialogue of St. Catherine of Siena,* St. Catherine of Siena

Servant of God Julia Greeley

- *In Secret Service of the Sacred Heart: The Life & Virtues of Julia Greeley,* Blaine Burkey
- See also: juliagreeley.org

Women of the French Revolution

- *Women and the Limits of Citizenship in the French Revolution,* Olwen H. Hufton
- *To Quell the Terror: The Mystery of the Vocation of the Sixteen Carmelites of Compiègne,* William Bush
- *Song of the Scaffold,* Gertrude von Le Fort

For Further Growth

If you are looking for more ways to cultivate a specific gift, here are a few ideas to get you started. Remember: While women are the "privileged sign" of these gifts, in the end, they are human gifts, so yes, men can, and should, grow in these areas, too!

Self-Giving and Generosity

- Always have a meal in your freezer that you can offer to a family in need
- Set up automatic contributions to your parish and favorite charities
- Volunteer
- When you encounter the homeless, shake their hand, introduce yourself, and ask them for their name
- Keep bags filled with essentials, such as water, soft foods, travel-sized hygiene products, and hand warmers, in your car to pass out to the homeless
- Spend five more minutes in prayer, especially when you do not want to
- If someone asks for your help, do it with a smile and try to give them a little more than they asked for

Receptivity

- Host a dinner club, small group, or Bible study in your home
- Learn more about the Holy Spirit and how to grow closer to him
- Enter into the sufferings the Lord allows and the blessings that he gives
- Use the phrase "just a minute" less often so you can receive others more quickly

- At a social gathering, if you sense that someone is trying to join your conversation, readily invite him or her in
- Create a guest room in your home (or at least have a blowup mattress ready) so you are always prepared to welcome guests
- Try not to complain. By not complaining, you say yes to the Lord in everything he gives you

Maternity

- Learn first aid and become CPR certified so you can be prepared to take care of others in a crisis
- Offer to watch someone else's children
- Seek to be a mentor to someone
- Teach religious education in your parish
- Volunteer for your parish day care center
- Offer to teach your unique skills to others
- Pray for those whom you spiritually mentor
- Get to know your neighbors and seek ways to serve them
- Visit older people in your community

Sensitivity and Intuition

- Volunteer to help during crises
- Lead a Bible study at a local jail or halfway house
- Look people in the eye when they talk to you
- Try to put yourself in the shoes of others and see a situation from their perspective
- Go on a mission trip
- Write thank you notes and recognize others for their contributions

- While waiting in line, ask someone near you how their day is going
- When you notice someone is in distress, seek to discern his or her need and help

Fidelity

- Do not cancel appointments unless it is a true emergency
- When you commit to a new job, volunteer position, move, or small group, set a minimum amount of time you will remain in that station before considering moving on and stick to it (unless the situation is unhealthy)
- Complete a long-term goal, such as writing a book, making a quilt, reading the whole Bible, etc.
- Read a challenging work of literature or Church document
- Set a daily prayer time and commit to it

Strength

- Prove to yourself that you are stronger than you think by participating in endurance activities such as long-distance running or biking.
- Go to counseling to grow in interior strength through healing if appropriate
- Admit when you are wrong and apologize
- Pray the Stations of the Cross and allow yourself to accompany the Lord with intention
- Stand up for the vulnerable in public situations

Bibliography

Allen, RSM, Sister Prudence. *The Concept of Woman: Volume III: The Search for Communion of Persons, 1500–2015.* Grand Rapids: William B. Eerdmans Publishing Company, 2016.

Burkey, Blaine. *An Hour with Julia Greeley.* Liguori, MO: Liguori Publications, 2020.

Burkey, Blaine. *In Secret Service of the Sacred Heart: The Life and Virtues of Julia Greeley.* Denver, CO: Julia Greeley Guild, 2012.

Bush, William. *To Quell the Terror.* Washington, DC: ICS Publications, 1999.

Catherine of Siena. *The Letters of St. Catherine of Siena: Volume 1.* Translated by Suzanne Noffke, OP. Medieval & Renaissance Texts & Studies, 1988.

Cathey, Alexandra Richards. "Unlocking the Feminine Genius with Edith Stein." Masters thesis, Holy Apostles College and Seminary, 2017.

Catholic Church. *Catechism of the Catholic Church.* 2nd ed. Washington, DC: United States Catholic Conference, 1997.

Day, Dorothy. *The Long Loneliness.* New York: Harper and Brothers, 1952.

Desan, Suzanne. 1989. "The Role of Women in Religious Riots During the French Revolution." *Eighteenth-Century Studies* 22, no. 3 (Spring 1989): 451–468. https://doi.org/10.2307/2738896.

Herbstrith, Waltraud. *Edith Stein: The Untold Story of the Philosopher and Mystic Who Lost Her Life in the Death Camps of Auschwitz.* Translated by Bernard Bonowitz. San Francisco: Ignatius Press, 1985.

Hufton, Olwen H. *Women and the Limits of Citizenship in the French Revolution.* Toronto: University of Toronto Press, 2015.

John Paul II. *Letter to Women.* Vatican website. June, 29, 1995.

John Paul II. *Mulieris Dignitatem.* Apostolic Letter. Vatican website. August 15, 1988.

John Paul II. *Pope John Paul II Speaks on Women.* Edited by Brooke Williams Deely. Washington DC: The Catholic University of America Press, 2014.

John Paul II. *Redemptoris Mater.* Encyclical Letter. Vatican website. March 25, 1987.

Leonard, Amy. *Nails in the Wall: Catholic Nuns in Reformation Germany.* Chicago: The University of Chicago Press, 2005.

O'Donnell, Catherine. *Elizabeth Seton: American Saint.* Ithaca: Cornell University Press, 2018.

Raymond of Capua. *The Life of St. Catherine of Siena.* Translated by George Lamb. Charlotte, NC: TAN Books, 1934.

Seton, Elizabeth Ann. *Elizabeth Bayley Seton: Collected Writings: Volume 1.* Edited by Regina Bechtle. Hyde Park, NY: New City Press, 2000.

Seton, Elizabeth Ann. *Elizabeth Bayley Seton: Collected Writings: Volume 2.* Edited by Regina Bechtle. Hyde Park, NY: New City Press, 2002.

Stein, Edith. *Essays on Women.* Translated by Freda Mary Oben, PhD. Washington, DC: ISC Publications, 2017.

Stein, Edith. *Self Portrait in Letters: 1916-1942.* Edited by Dr. L. Gelber and Romaeus Leuven, OCD. Translated by Josephine Koeppel, OCD. Washington, DC: ISC Publications, 1993.

Troisi, Simone, and Cristiana Paccini. *Chiara Corbella Petrillo: A Witness to Joy.* Manchester, NH: Sophia Institute Press, 2015.

Vogt, Brandon. *Saints and Social Justice: A Guide to Changing the World.* Huntington, IN: Our Sunday Visitor, 2014.

von Le Fort, Gertrud. *The Eternal Woman.* San Francisco: Ignatius Press, 2010.

Wright, Terrence C. *Dorothy Day: An Introduction to Her Life and Thought.* San Francisco: Ignatius Press, 2018.

Acknowledgments

Thank you to the women of my feminine genius study:
Alison, Currie, Christina, Emmy, Ewelina, Katy, Katie, Sarah M.,
Sarah T., and Rachel. I cherish the memories of our study nights and am
so thankful for your sharing your experience of womanhood with me.
Your insights and influence are written throughout these pages.

Thank you to Madi Abbot, Rachel Bertotti, and Sister Cecilia Rose
for reviewing my manuscript's rough draft. Your time and attention
to this project were a true gift. I hope you reread it to see how
your feedback made the book even better!

Thank you to the many historians and experts who reviewed this content
for accuracy: Sister Tatum McWhirter, AVI, Dr. Catherine O'Donnell,
Dr. Elizabeth Mitchel, Dr. Terrance Wright, Dr. Bronwen McShea,
Dr. Greg Bottaro, and Mary Leisring. I am incredibly grateful
for your years of study that you share with the world.

Thank you to the team at Ascension for all their dedicated efforts
in making this book a reality.

Thank you to my husband and children for your patience throughout
this process. The sacrifices you made for the sake of this project
did not go unnoticed. I love you all the day.

Thank you to God the Father, Son, and Holy Spirit. May all glory
be given to you as a result of the book.

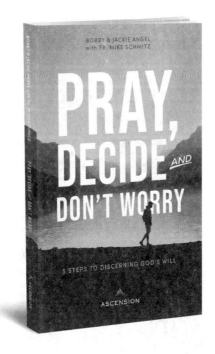

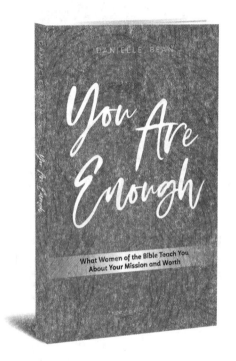